What They're Say...
Don't Just Give i...

Every once in a while a book comes along which, though written with down-to-earth clarity and simplicity, carries within its covers a clarion call to reverse the flow of power and unsettle the status quo in an entire facet of society. This is that book.
> —Stephen B. Nill, J.D., Editor
> *American Philanthropy Review*

Don't Just Give It Away is a great little book ... I wish (it) had been written years earlier—I could have used it.
> —Paul Newman
> from the Foreword

Don't Just Give It Away is a very special book, and it made clear to us how vital it is to have a focus if we are to have a real impact through philanthropy.
> —Robert Wagner
> —Jill St. John Wagner

As one who has spent his adult life in philanthropy, I applaud Mrs. Rafferty. This book is an essential guideline for any person, family or corporation wishing to become heavily involved in humanitarian causes.
> —Monty Hall, Life Chairman
> International Variety Children's Charities

Fascinating ... I couldn't put it down! It is THE bible on how to give responsibly.
> —Doris Buffett Bryant
> Founder-President
> The Sunshine Foundation

Indispensable and iconoclastic ... *Don't Just Give It Away* gores the 'sacred cows' of charity and philanthropy as we traditionally think of them.
> —Peter B. Manzo
> Executive Director
> Center for Nonprofit Management
> of Southern California

An invaluable primer and resource for anyone involved in the preservation of wealth and the stewardship of philanthropic endeavors.
—Kent Williams, Senior Vice President
U.S. Trust Company, N.A.

Practical and savvy advice for donors of all ages, interests, and capacities to give ... *Don't Just Give It Away* celebrates the joy of giving while bringing perspective and light to a subject that needed to be demystified.
—William P. Massey, President
National Charities Information Bureau

(It) forced me to examine my own beliefs about the role I play in society.
—Paula Parker-Sawyers
Former Executive Director
The Association of Black Foundation Executives

Using this book—and it is a book to be used—will have at least two consequences: your charitable giving will be more effective, and the organizations you support will be better served.
—Maurice Hodgen, Executive Director
The Community Foundation of Riverside County

A thought-provoking expose presenting realistic and practical strategies on how the giver can be a force for change.
—Lu Molberg, President
The Webster Institute

Don't Just Give It Away makes it brilliantly clear: 'business as usual' shouldn't—and won't—cut it with funders anymore.
—Carlos Martinez, Executive Director
La Alianza Hispana

This is the one book that every grantmaker, grantseeker, and trustee should keep at hand—I will.
—Judy Vossler, President
V!VA Foundation

Renata Rafferty makes you think about the things that are important in your life and future ... She is an outstanding professional in philanthropy.
> —Chadwick Mooney
> Senior Vice President - Investments
> Director's Council, Salomon Smith Barney

Mrs. Rafferty's experience and perspective are beautifully presented using commonsense language and practical tips.
> —Virginia Esposito, President
> National Center for Family Philanthropy

The message she communicates is simple, direct, useful and applicable. The book both fascinated and educated me.
> —Jo Ann Resch McGrath, Chair
> Highland Street Connection, a Family Foundation

Thoroughly engaging ... *Don't Just Give It Away* makes the philanthropic process a clear, simple, and meaningful one.
> —Ruth Goodan Applegarth
> The Applegarth Trust

This is the book her audiences have been asking for over the past ten years ... they won't be disappointed!
> —Patricia Gribow, Founder & Principal
> Proscenium International Speakers Bureau

Don't Just Give It Away

How to Make the Most of Your Charitable Giving

Renata J. Rafferty

Chandler House Press
Worcester, Massachusetts

ISBN 1-886284-32-6
Library of Congress Catalog Card Number 98-89747
First Edition
ABCDEFGHIJK

Published by
Chandler House Press
335 Chandler Street
Worcester, MA 01602 USA

President
Lawrence J. Abramoff

Publisher/Editor-in-Chief
Richard J. Staron

Editorial/Production Manager
Jennifer J. Goguen

Director of Retail Sales and Marketing
Claire Cousineau Smith

Book Design and Production
CWL Publishing Enterprises
3010 Irvington Way
Madison, WI 53713 USA
www.execpc.com/cwlpubent

Chandler House Press books are available at special discounts for bulk purchases. For more information about how to arrange such purchases, please contact Chandler House Press, 335 Chandler Street, Worcester, MA 01602, or call (800) 642-6657, or fax (508) 756-9425, or find us on the World Wide Web at www.tatnuck.com.

Chandler House Press books are distributed to the trade by
National Book Network
4720 Boston Way
Lanham, MD 20706
(800) 462-6420

Contents

Contents

Acknowledgments

riting a book is a daunting task—particularly when you hope to break new ground and expose new perspectives in a way that just might provoke change in our world.

Many individuals conspired to force me to the keyboard to share what has become the focus for my professional life—reintroducing passion, hope, vision, and critical analysis to the philanthropic process. And bringing joy back into the dynamic that motivates one to place a "bet" on others.

First, I would like to thank Dr. Arthur Bloom, Dr. Carol Kauffman, and Ms. Sharon Baker for their work in building the foundation that would allow me to teach, to write, and to lead in this field.

A unique collection of women—unknown even to one another—wove a safety net of sanity for me during the writing of this book: my assistants Donna Ricketson and Ellie Weiner, who kept the field cleared for writing time; Patricia Gribow, head of Proscenium, the speakers bureau that represents me, for inspiring me to translate the spoken language of philanthropy to the written word; Jan Fraser of the Gannett Corporation, who was the first business editor of a daily newspaper in this country to recognize the importance of the "business" of philanthropy—and backed it up by running my column; and Judy Vossler, who can administer the kindest kick in the butt of almost anyone I know.

Over the years, Linda Kuczma has been there for me in every way one could hope of one's closest friend. With respect to this book, she took on another responsibility, that of acting as my attorney. As a respected expert in the field of intellectual property law, she and her firm, Wallenstein & Wagner Ltd. of Chicago, ensured that I did not "just give it away."

I must especially thank Patty Newman (and her Arthur) for calling on her family's support for this project.

Without Pegine Echevarria, this book—truly—would never have been written or published. As one of the nation's leading authorities on mentoring, she practices what she preaches. After we both spoke at a conference in Toronto, she insisted on introducing me to her publisher, and has been there for me throughout this project.

That publisher, Dick Staron of Chandler House Press, took a risk in bringing a book on philanthropy to the general market. Authors of books of this sort are usually resigned to publishing for "the trade," with little hope that their work will gain access to the public at large. Dick understood that with 11% of this country's economy tied to the nonprofit sector, it was imperative that the public have access to the information and guidance offered by this book. His belief in the book was echoed by everyone at Chandler House, from Jennifer Goguen, Production Manager, to Claire Cousineau Smith, Director of Retail Sales, to Lawrence Abramoff, President of Chandler House Press (and a philanthropist).

The spirit of this book, however, traces its roots to one very special person in the charitable sector—Joseph Tobin, Vice President of External Affairs for Eisenhower Medical Center in California. Joe's dry humor and kind spirit has touched—and moved—a dynasty of philanthropists whose names would be instantly recognizable the world over. As neighbor, friend, and mentor, however, he somehow was able to find time for simple me. His generosity with introductions and advice could always be counted on, even if it meant taking a gentle jibe now and then as the price.

Everyone always thanks their family—usually just for being there, and for continuing to love us as we become more insufferable through the writing process. In that respect, my small family contributed enormously to this project.

But they played such a larger role in the writing of this book that I would be remiss not to acknowledge their contributions individually.

My mother and late father, Irene and Chester Daroszewski came to this country after World War II with an unshakable faith in the American dream. But the dream was not one of wealth, it was one of freedom ... the freedom expressed through the words "life, liberty, and the pursuit of happiness." For me, philanthropy—the love of humanity—is rooted in the freedom my parents sought, and found, on these shores.

I counted on someone who is a far better writer than me (or is it I?) as in-house critic, editor, and—when I was completely over-whelmed—court jester, my dear sister Barbara Daroszewski. Her tales of adventure from the Slavic tundra reminded me daily of the beauty of language and the importance of being precise. I look forward to returning the favor on her book.

My deepest gratitude, however, has been and always will be for Jerome Howes Rafferty. Unconditional love usually comes as part of the marital package. Unconditional respect does not. His respect for me as a human, as a woman, as a professional shows itself abundantly and on a daily basis—and from that respect came the courage to speak out, and write, about philanthropy and the passion to make change in the world. Thank you.

Foreword
by Paul Newman

If someone asked me whether I was raised to be a "philan-thropist," I'd probably have to say no. But as I look back and think about what messages I grew up with in my home, I'd have to say I was raised to think about the needs of the people around me.

My brother Arthur and I grew up in Shaker Heights, Ohio. My father and my Uncle Joe owned the largest sporting goods store in the state. What a great business for a kid's dad to be in! Unless, of course, it's 1929 and the country is entering the worst Depression of its history.

As you can imagine, trying to move sporting goods while peo-ple were desperately trying to keep food on the table was not an easy proposition. Other men might have walked away or folded until times were better and people were in a position to start buy-ing skis or skates or footballs again.

But not my father and uncle. They felt an obligation to the people who worked for them and to their families. Amazingly, not one of their employees was let go from work during the Depression. It wasn't until I was much older that I could appreci-ate the lengths to which my father and uncle went to insure that everyone at Newman-Stern stayed employed during that terrible time.

My mother's brand of caring—as you might expect from a "mom"—was somewhat more hands-on. To give you an example, each Christmas Eve while we were growing up, she would take Arthur and me to the family's store to gather up toys and equipment to take to our Hungarian relatives on the other side of town. That annual "Christmas expedition" became the heart of our holiday ritual.

So, can I say that my parents sat me down and showed me how to care, how to make charity a guiding principle in my life, how to be a philanthropist? Not really. But I did learn that caring only about oneself and one's immediate family is not enough when you are in a position to help others. And I learned it by example.

As an actor, I've often been asked to describe the process of creating a character. Acting is a question of absorbing other people's personalities and adding some of your own experience. If I had to describe philanthropy, I'd say the process is just the reverse. You start with your own experiences and from there you grow to embrace the needs of others.

In our office at Newman's Own, there's a brass plaque that reads "Assistant Life Guard on Duty." Like so much in this enterprise, it was hung as a joke. But there's a lot of truth there about our company's mission.

Philanthropy is about safeguarding and honoring life. It's about getting beyond ourselves and connecting with our "global family." Yet the simple, pure act of giving is so unusual today that people are baffled by it, and we wind up thinking it's more complicated than it really is.

Don't Just Give It Away is a great little book. It brings our understanding of the act of philanthropy back to its simplest roots, and reinforces that very human impulse within each of us to take better care of each other.

More than that, *Don't Just Give It Away* teaches us how to act on that giving impulse in a responsible and objective manner – with a view toward making a lasting difference.

A significant portion of Newman's Own charitable contributions have gone into setting up recreational camps for seriously ill children all around the world. If I ever had a doubt about whether this was an "investment" that made sense, that doubt is long gone. You create something where the children are to be the ben-eficiaries and find out that you get back a great deal more than you give.

No, I never planned to become a philanthropist. But it has been a tremendous ride—one that I'm proud to say my family has joined me on. I learned by the seat of my pants—and on the strength of a salad dressing that surprised itself into a corporate empire.

I wish *Don't Just Give It Away* had been written years earlier—I could have used it. I'm delighted that it's here now and that I can share this book with friends, family, and colleagues who are searching for their own ways—more personal ways—to make this world a better place through wiser charitable giving.

Paul Newman's accomplishments as an Academy Award-winning actor and successful race car driver have been eclipsed in recent years by his astonishing innovation in the field of philanthropy. In 1982, he founded Newman's Own, a for-profit food products corpo-ration that donates fully 100% of its after-tax profits to charities around the globe. To date, the company's contributions total well over $100 million worldwide.

In memory of
Edward R. Daroszewski
and
Klara Plawinska
A scholar and a saint

Preface

What total amount would you guess is donated to charity in any given year?

**In 1997 alone, Americans contributed
$143 billion to nonprofit organizations.**

**Individuals and families donated
$122 billion of that in direct gifts or bequests.**

Do these staggering numbers surprise you? They should! Look around our communities, and across the nation as a whole—does it seem that $143 billion of "social progress" was achieved through the activities of the charitable sector? How much of that $143 billion did you and your family contribute, and do you believe it was used as wisely as it could have been?

Having worked and consulted within the charitable sector for over twenty years, I have witnessed the integrity and industry of the men and women of this sector who commit their lives—professionally or as volunteers—to make this world a better place for all of us.

Unfortunately, I could also tell you stories of waste and poor financial management that substantially eroded the value of our contributions—stories that never surface in the press or through the grapevine for fear that we will reconsider our charitable support.

In fact, I can guarantee that if you've ever made a charitable contribution, at least some small portion of that gift could probably have been used a little more effectively by the organization to which you gave it. Perhaps another charity would have accom plished a great deal more. And sadly, in some cases we might just as well have thrown our money away.

Like a leaking faucet that accumulates in wasted gallons, minor misuses of each of our charitable investments add up. In fact, they amount to huge amounts of donated money annually that could have—and should have—been applied to programs and services for the community ... but weren't. And that's why we don't see $143 billion worth of progress from our contributions.

In the very best cases, that "leakage" of funds causes an organization to do just a little less than it otherwise could. In the worst cases, vital and urgent human needs of real-life men, women, and children are going unmet—needs such as food, clothing, shelter, good health, education, and safety—because no one in the organization is truly "minding the store." Most cases fall somewhere in between.

How will this change? How can we as a community get our money's worth for our charitable contributions?

Nonprofits Must Change

First, the nonprofit sector—collectively and as individual charitable corporations—must take its critical role in society far more seriously. This is particularly true for the volunteer leaders who are entrusted as board directors and trustees—the legal, financial, and moral guardians of our charitable sector.

And this is happening. The nonprofit community has looked at itself in the mirror (and in *The Wall Street Journal*, *Forbes*, *Fortune*, and *The Economist*) and has redoubled its efforts—particularly since the United Way scandal of a few years back—to become more accountable, more professional, and more effective.

The government is also doing its share in this effort. The Taxpayer Bill of Rights has made it obligatory for the majority of charities to share their financial information upon demand. And, with backup from the IRS, government has forced boards and administrators to approach issues of compensation, self-dealing, and conflict of interest with greater deliberation.

Nonprofit leaders, too are applying themselves to strengthening the sector through professional development. They are increasingly seeking technical assistance and education—training in nonprofit management, fund development, governance, strategic planning, program development, and outcomes evaluation. In fact, academic degree and certification programs in fundraising and philanthropic administration are flourishing.

And finally—slowly but surely—board trustees are approaching their fiduciary responsibilities with ever greater seriousness.

We as Donors Must Change

But the bottom line is still ... the "bottom line." Whoever controls the bottom line has the greatest power—perhaps the greatest responsibility—when it comes to effecting constructive change.

And in the charitable sector, it is donors, givers, and philanthropists who ultimately control the bottom line. If you give to charity, you have the power to make the charitable sector more effective.

There is value in most every type and amount of charitable contribution. The more wisely the giving decision is made, the more valuable—and effective—is the gift.

To donate wisely—and therefore more effectively—we must take better control of our giving, and assess "charitable investment" opportunities as carefully as we would any other financial investment opportunity.

By working more closely with the nonprofit community, and making our giving choices more critically, we as individual donors and philanthropists can:

- Increase the economic impact of both our personal and combined charitable contributions
- Improve the quality of life in our communities and around the world, and
- Find a deeper personal satisfaction in charitable giving than we ever imagined.

This book will show you how.

Part One

Giving, Charity, and Philanthropy: There Is a Difference

Introduction

Why a Guide to "Philanthropy"?

❦

*Oh, Pookie, you're going to have such a hell of a lot
of fun with the foundation when I'm gone.*
—Vincent to Brooke Astor before his death

❦

What is the most satisfying giving experience you've ever had? Having asked this question hundreds of times over the last two decades, the varied responses still never fail to amaze and move me. Yet I am struck by how very, very rarely these highly personal stories involve conventional forms of giving to charitable organizations.

Ironically, many of the individuals least satisfied by their charitable giving are among the most prominent, visible, and generous financial contributors to nonprofits within their communities.

How is it that hundreds of billions of dollars are being channeled to charities world-wide each year by millions of donors, and yet so few donors feel a deep and abiding satisfaction from their financial contribution?

Put more simply, why does it seem like no one is having much fun in philanthropy anymore?

Yes, there are lots of galas, auctions, raffles, car washes, and cookie-thons. And a great deal of pleasure is had by all—in fact, it's such a good time, you'd hardly know it was "charitable" at all! Like "fat free" ice cream, we enjoy it despite the fact that it's supposed to be good for us.

A Change in Meaning

When society used to speak of "philanthropy," economic barons from another era—like Andrew Carnegie—would come to mind. And we could point to a concrete impact they had on our world— forging a nationwide library system, for example.

Over time, however, there has been a subtle shift in our notion of a philanthropist. We still identify philanthropists as a class of "economic barons." but we find it a little harder to identify exactly what they have accomplished for society. And we have come to question their motives.

In fact, today's cynics would have us believe that a "philanthropist" is typically a stock-wealthy social statesmen (white and older, of course) who thinks he knows what's better for all of us.

Or put another way, a "philanthropist" is anyone with "a lot of money" who gives some of it away—and if they score a few PR points for themselves, all the better.

Depending, then, on how you define "a lot of money" and whether you give any of it away, you've probably already decided whether you are or could ever be a "philanthropist."

I've written this book to remind all of us that *anyone* can be a philanthropist, in the truest meaning of the word—and that being a philanthropist can and should be one of the most genuinely human and satisfying experiences or aspects of life. For—to paraphrase Millie Thornton—philanthropy is a *principle*, not an amount.

How to begin? This book will show you *how* to become a philanthropist, from A to Z, regardless of your economic means.

What This Book Is NOT

This book is NOT intended to convince anyone of the importance or value of giving. That is a decision that you have already arrived at alone, with your family, with your fellow board members, or with your legal and financial advisors.

This book is *not* about the various legal structures or vehicles through which philanthropic gifts can be made. It is not about the financial incentives of philanthropy for high-net-worth individuals. It is not about building better community relations—even global community relations—through targeted corporate philanthropy.

This book is *not* designed to lead you to give more or less generously, or to more or fewer causes, or to any specific causes, or to change your mind about the giving in which you are already engaged.

So What IS This Book About?

If you are going to give to charity, you should give with enthusiasm and derive a great deal of heart-felt satisfaction in the act, because through philanthropy you do make the world a better place for all.

But when it comes to making your charitable investments, don't just *give* it away!

This book is about approaching philanthropic giving as thoughtfully and insightfully—and personally—as you approach your financial investing.

This book is about a personal redefinition of philanthropy.

And, it is about learning how to give with genuine enthusiasm—an enthusiasm rooted in the conviction that you can provoke positive, meaningful change in this world!

In essence, it is about making a fundamental change in the role you, your family, or your business play in your community and in the family of mankind.

Back to the "Real World"

❦

Giving away money effectively
is almost as hard as earning it in the first place.
—Bill Gates

❦

If you're tempted to stop reading, let me reassure you—this is no "Zen and the Art of Giving." It is a practical, "how to" primer.

You've been careful in securing your future and that of your business—now what will you do with the rest of the money? This book will teach you how to make as careful an "investment" decision with your charitable giving as you have in your personal financial planning.

How Do I Know if This Book Is for Me?

Whether you are newly committed to the idea of philanthropy, or looking for greater satisfaction from your charitable giving, or seeking assurance that your contributions are being used as effectively as possible, this book IS for you.

If you still have any doubts, review these stories of other folks who found the information in this book helpful *and* inspiring. Perhaps you'll meet someone whose story parallels your own:

1. Your financial consultant or legal advisor has urged you to "get charitable" as a means of preserving your wealth, reducing your tax liability, or passing assets to your heirs intact.

Bill and Marilyn*, a wonderful couple in their late 60s, were advised by their financial consultant that the establishment of a charitable remainder trust could solve their capital gains dilemma on a portfolio of highly appreciated stock. Moreover, the trust arrangement would accommodate the purchase of replacement life insurance that would guarantee their children's receipt of the

---

*Unless available through public sources, the names of individuals whose stories are told in this book, as well as any distinctly identifying information, have been changed in order to respect their privacy and the privacy of their families.

equivalent full value of their parents' estate upon Bill's and Marilyn's deaths.

The couple's estate planning attorney drew up the necessary documents, but when it came time for them to name a required beneficiary charity, they were lost. They had been so busy working and raising their family that they had never had the opportunity to get involved in charity, and now were being asked to donate the fruits of their life's work to one of hundreds of thousands of causes. Using the guidelines in this book, Bill and Marilyn were able to uncover a shared passion for a little-known cause. Childhood sweethearts, they decided to honor the town where they met and grew up by selecting a charity in that community. They followed the steps outlined in this book to assure themselves that their chosen charity had sound leadership and fiscal stability.

The unexpected satisfaction they experienced through this process inspired Bill and Marilyn to become involved with charitable work in their retirement community, something they never would have considered before.

2. Your wise career choice and the wild success of your employer—or your own business—has placed you in a position of financial comfort you never imagined. In gratitude for your good fortune, you would like to "give back" to the community.

Linda went to work for a go-go computer software manufacturer right out of college. Although her salary would never make her "rich," she took advantage of the firm's generous employee stock option program. Eighteen years later, she was able to retire from the publicly traded company. Having experienced the advantages of working in the technology industry, Linda decided that she wanted to apply some of her wealth to help at-risk kids access the opportunities of the computer field.

Where to start? Virtually every city and town in the country has a youth population in need. Should she apply her resources to groups working with children, teens, or young adults? Was it education, career information, or networking opportunities that would help fast-track Linda's successors into the field that had been so generous to her? By utilizing the tools and guides in this book,

Linda was able to focus on those critical events in her own life that had opened the door for her to high-tech, and she was able to make clear decisions about how to use her charitable investment to help others step through that door, too.

3. You have been involved in charitable giving for years, and are finding less and less satisfaction in sponsoring tables at the gala, holes at the golf tournament, or rooms in new buildings.

Norm and his wife Marguerite live the comfortable country club life of many retired corporate executives. A generous pension, stock options, and very wise investing have given them the freedom to travel around the globe, and to entertain frequently at both their Midwest and Palm Springs homes. Norm's large network of top-level business colleagues, coupled with Marguerite's high social profile, place them at the top of every charity's A-list.

About five years into retirement, Norm and Marguerite changed financial advisors. It was then that Norm and Marguerite realized, for the first time really, how much they had given over the years to charity, primarily through event sponsorships, silent and live auctions, charity sports tournaments, naming opportunities in new buildings, and countless ticket purchases to events they hadn't even attended. Norm, particularly, was astounded. He realized he never would have made business investment decisions the way he and Marguerite had been making their charitable investments.

They decided as a couple that they had endured enough balls, auctions, and tournaments to last a lifetime. It was time to invest their contributions in a more business-like manner. As charity was a new "business" to both Norm and Marguerite, they sought the professional counsel of their financial advisor and the guidance offered in this book to restructure their charitable giving.

Norm now understands that the profit and nonprofit worlds are not so far apart: market assessment, strategic planning, committed and knowledgeable leadership, quality programs and service, relevant evaluation methodologies, and sound fiscal and investment policies are the hallmark of every successful nonprofit. Norm is enjoying applying an investment perspective in making the final family giving decisions while Marguerite has learned how better to listen to her heart in setting the family's charitable course.

4. You receive many more requests for contributions than you could possibly respond to positively—you would like to say "no" without feeling guilty.

Nancy's name recently appeared in a local publication as one of the top philanthropists in her community. She had more requests than she could respond to even before the article came out. Now she is flooded with calls and letters, and most of the requests are for truly worthy causes. Nancy woke up many nights overwhelmed with guilt about all the people she couldn't help, and wondering how she could say "no" without feeling so badly about it. She reviewed the principles outlined in this book.

Once she understood why and how an effective philanthropist MUST say "no," and how to make the wisest decision about how and when to say "yes," Nancy was able to become a more powerful force for positive change in her community—gaining admirers and emulators in the process.

5. Your family or business has decided to consolidate its charitable giving through the establishment of a foundation.

Ed had built a multi-national corporation through a brilliant strategy of acquisitions and mergers. Over the years, many organizations in the company's home town had asked for contributions for a local cause. Early on, the requests had come to Ed's office directly, and he'd often write a check out of his own account. Soon, Ed became too busy to deal with non-business-related matters, and had his secretary pass requests for help to the human resources manager.

As the company grew, human resources could no longer deal with charity pleas, and the responsibility was turned over to the new community relations department. Now, the requests no longer came from just the home office community. With each new merger or acquisition, charities from those communities joined the ranks of those applying for funding. With no cohesive policy on giving, there was no way to track whether the gifts served or supported the company's mission, or whether the funds even had any truly positive impact on the community.

In the interest of good corporate citizenship, Ed and his board of directors decided to consolidate the company's giving activities through the establishment of a corporate charitable foundation. Through the foundation, the firm is now making substantial grants that benefit the communities around the world where their employees and clients live and work. They have been able to link nonprofits from different communities to share innovative approaches, and through targeted funding have facilitated collaborations on a local level. Most importantly for Ed, the foundation serves as a focal point of unity, strength, and a common mission for the many diverse divisions and cultures represented in his multi-national operation. The principles and approaches outlined in this book shaped that corporate foundation.

6. Your spouse or partner used to receive and handle all of the requests for contributions—it's now become your responsibility.

Barbara and Barry ran a successful business operation that grew to a multi-entity corporation. Over the eighteen years of their marriage, they made many charitable contributions. Barry, as the more visible partner in the business, received most of the requests and made most of the giving decisions. An ugly divorce resulted in a split of the business. Barry bought out Barbara's share.

Word spread that her settlement was large, and Barbara became a prime target for charities throughout the community. She was besieged by requests for money and time, requests she had never handled before. Her financial advisors offered little guidance in this area, often suggesting that Barbara merely follow the patterns of giving that Barry had established. Barbara needed to take some time to re-examine her personal priorities and get acquainted with the work and needs of the charities approaching her. Then she had to start making some tough financial decisions about which groups to support. The principles in this book guided her through this process.

7. You sit on numerous charity boards and are asked to serve on many more than you can accommodate. You would like to ensure that your investment of time, energy, expertise, and money is directed where it can have the greatest impact.

Monica's family name is well-known nationally in both the business and the charity communities. Many nonprofits have asked Monica to serve on their boards, promising that little would be expected of her, given her hectic schedule. These charities believe that just having Monica's name on the letterhead would bring credibility—and hopefully a contribution from her family's coffers—to the organization. Once Monica realized that spreading her name so thinly diluted its value to all of the charities, she decided to pare back and give her full attention—and generous financial support—to only two nonprofits per year. She asked each organization to prepare, in essence, a proposal for her support. Using the information and questions in this book, she made an objective selection of her first two beneficiaries, and has continued to play an important role in the accomplishments of those two groups ever since.

8. You recognized yourself as "the millionaire next door"—and realized that charity that "starts at home and stays at home" may harm your children more than it helps.

Jim and Florence married when he returned from WW II's Pacific theater. Jim worked as a teacher and Florence as a secretary. They raised two sons and a daughter, all the while dutifully putting 15% of their earnings in savings. When Florence's parents died, they left their estate—including a home and some investments—to Jim and Flo. The couple decided that hard work, their focus on family, and shared goals and values were the greatest legacy they could pass to their children. They were concerned that passing the windfall to their offspring, now in their 30s, would deprive the young people of the opportunity to find their own paths and meet their own challenges, as Jim and Florence had.

They made arrangements for the eventual financial comfort of their children, and then decided to invest in charities that would benefit their grandchildren. Not knowing where to start, they took the steps outlined in this book to guide them.

9. Your recent lottery win, inheritance, or appearance in a major publication has brought a flood of requests for charitable contributions and you do not know how to respond or react.

Sharon's fast-growing homemade food company was featured on the business page of the city newspaper. Overnight, community groups from throughout that region of the state began writing and calling to request sponsorship funds and program grants—

from food banks to Girl Scout troops. She knew that some of these organizations could help bring her company even more recognition—and sales—but wasn't sure how to guarantee that her company got the mileage she wanted from these charitable contributions. The tips in this book helped her understand what to look—and ask—for.

10. You have no heirs, and would like to use your fortune to leave a meaningful legacy.

Ruth had never married and had no children. As an only child with virtually no extended family, she realized that with her passing, the family name would vanish. She decided to leave her estate to a charity that would agree to name a room or building wing in her family's honor. Where to start? In the port city that welcomed her immigrant parents, her current home town, the city where she had attended college? How did one go about finding a building looking for a name? How could she be sure the name would continue to be used? The step-by-step question-and-answer format of this book led Ruth to her answer.

Before You Begin...

This book provides a comprehensive guide to defining your personal, family, or corporate philanthropic focus. It also outlines a step-by-step process for identifying and assessing charitable organizations and programs that meet the philanthropic guidelines that you develop.

The manner in which you choose to structure, convey, or time a charitable gift is not a subject for this book. That is a matter best discussed and determined with your professional financial and legal advisors.

I invite you to look at philanthropy in a whole new light.

Chapter 1

Giving and Getting

❦

*Giving should be entered
into in just the same careful way as investing ....
Giving is investing.*
—John D. Rockefeller

❦

Investing in charity is no different from investing in the market. It is a proactive process of defining your investment goals and identifying opportunities that will lead to those goals.

Yet a substantial amount of "charitable giving" today is approached as casually as the purchase of a lottery ticket. The brief satisfaction of the contribution outweighs whether or not any specific or measurable "investment" goal was achieved.

A lottery ticket may cost only $1. But many philanthropic donations made today range from less than $100 to well over $1 million—with shockingly little attention paid to real outcomes.

In 1997—in the U.S. alone—nearly 650,000 charities solicited and secured over $150 billion in contributions from individuals and corporations. Did the donors get their money's worth? To put it more personally, did you get your money's worth? And how would you know whether you did?

What did you expect to result from your gift? What did you expect as an outcome? Much of that will depend on what motivated you to to give.

Who Gives and Why?

Charitable donors can generally be separated into four major categories: the "social" donor, the "quid pro quo" donor, the "conscience" donor, and the true philanthropist.

The Social Donor

The social donor—also known among fund-raisers as the "vanity" giver—places a high value on the personal visibility and prestige his or her contribution will bring. Such donors also place great importance on interacting with other high-profile community leaders and public figures. The fact that their funds may influence a constructive change in the community is secondary in the donor's evaluation of the investment.

In one example of a social gift, an East Coast newcomer to a high-net-worth retirement community on the West Coast contacted our firm for information on the major charities in this Southern California desert resort. When asked about his charitable interests, the gentleman replied he had none. He just wanted to get acquainted with the town's wealthy movers and shakers as quickly as possible and knew the charity route was the fastest way to accomplish that end.

Charitable gifts from this category are primarily mid-sized to very large—depending on who else is at the table. "I'll see you and raise you" is not an uncommon attitude. The expected return on investment is prominent recognition and the opportunity to socialize on a regular basis with contributors of similar social or economic class. Rarely does the donor require the nonprofit to "document" the institution's use of the "investment," or to report on the organization's performance as impacted by the contribution.

In another example, a major real estate developer was having difficulty in getting what he felt was a "fair hearing" on his controversial new project. He investigated the city councilpersons' charitable involvements and discovered that a majority of them happened to belong to a cultural institution's auxilliary group. He immediately "bought" a high-level membership in the support club. A key benefit of membership was frequent social gatherings and "preview" cocktail parties at which this small group of supporters could mingle and chat. It was the perfect opportunity for the developer to meet his adversaries informally and off-the-record to talk up the benefits of his project—while serving the charitable interests of the community at the same time. The developer, by the way, never cared what the organization did with his money. He felt he got what he paid for: access to individuals who would have a major influence on the success or failure of his business dealings.

The "Quid pro Quo" Giver

The second category of donor is the "quid pro quo" giver. These contributors generally donate to organizations in which a close friend or colleague is involved. The nature of the subject nonprofit is almost irrelevant. The contribution is based on a respect for or trust in the person making the request.

A few years back, I was sharing a working lunch with the capital campaign chair of a children's organization. We were dining at his private country club when an older gentleman approached our table and gave my companion a hearty greeting. When asked what the campaign chair was up to these days, he replied, "Oh, we're trying to build a new museum." As the gentleman continued to his own table, he remarked over his shoulder, "Put me down for fifty." In twenty years of experience, that was the fastest $50,000 commitment I'd ever witnessed. And it was made solely on the basis of the trust and respect felt for the capital campaign chairman.

In another type of quid pro quo gift situation, there is often the unspoken understanding that the donor may request a contribution for his or her own favorite charity in the future.

At more than one donor prospect rating meeting I've heard charity volunteers say, "I gave $10,000 to his pet charity, he owes me. I know I can get at least ten back out of him." In many circles, charitable contributions have become a social currency, a "debt marker" of sorts. And in these situations, as with vanity giving, return on investment is rarely measured in terms of organizational outcomes.

The "Social Conscience" Supporter

The third category of donor is the "social conscience" supporter. These are persons who give to one or more organizations because they truly and deeply believe in the importance or urgency of the nonprofit's mission. The donor may or may not have a personal connection with the agency, but will respond to a reasoned and impassioned request that touches his or her own concerns.

The most common form of conscience giving is via response to a direct mail request. Most often, the request will come from a well-established or highly credible charity, either national or very local in scope. It may be from the Sierra Club, the American Cancer Society, Amnesty International, or the local Cub Scout pack. The donor responds because of a general conviction that the work of the organization is vital, and that the leadership of the charity will use the contribution wisely—and there is a track record to support these assumptions.

A conscience contributor is not unlike the small-time investor who buys blue chip stock because he or she trusts—without knowing a lot of details—that it will perform well.

Despite general familiarity with the mission, conscience contributors can seldom list for you the specific initiatives or programs which are sponsored by the charity. And they rarely know—or particularly care—about exactly how their contribution was used or what measurable impact it had. This is true, in large part, because such a donation is usually relatively modest in size.

The Philanthropist

The final category of charitable contributor is the focus for this book—that is, the "philanthropist." In contemporary parlance, "philanthropist" has come to describe anyone of wealth who gives any of it to charity. What an injustice to the true philanthropist!

In short, philanthropists are those contributors who carefully invest their wealth in the nonprofit sector specifically in order to benefit the general good of humanity, and to effect substantive positive change in the world.

Unlike givers in the preceding three categories, the philanthropist—whose contribution may range from mid-size to megagift—will be most interested in how and to what degree his or her contribution has had a profound, lasting, and measurable impact on some particular social challenge.

The best-publicized gifts of contemporary philanthropy are those of enormous financial magnitude. A benchmark in philanthropy was set in 1995 when Walter Annenberg, former U.S. Ambassador to the Court of St. James, donated $500 million to public education in an effort to improve school systems nationwide.

More recently, broadcast magnate Ted Turner committed $1 billion over ten years to the United Nations in support of its worldwide relief and charitable activities. His philanthropic contribution had a double objective. Immediately apparent was the desire to improve the living conditions of the underserved and at-risk—particularly children—across the globe. Less obvious was his deliberate intent to provoke fellow billionaires, such as Bill Gates and Warren Buffett, to follow his philanthropic example.

To more fully understand the notion of philanthropy—or philanthropic investment—one needs to appreciate the fundamental differences between giving, charity, and philanthropy.

Giving, Charity, and Philanthropy

❦

Too many have dispensed with generosity in order to practice charity.

—Albert Camus

❦

Philanthropy is a state of mind—optimistic, determined, energized, and creative. Philanthropy is entrepreneurial. In fact, some of the world's most effective philanthropists were successful business entrepreneurs and visionaries. The same talents, insights, and drive that fueled their business success also made them great philanthropists.

Giving, charity, and philanthropy. These three words are often used interchangeably, yet even "charity" and "giving" have an unmistakable, albeit subtle, difference in meaning. And "philanthropy" is an act quite apart from either simple giving or charity, for *philanthropy demands results.*

Giving

What does it mean when we "give" something? We give it "away." The act of giving suggests the one-way transfer of a tangible or intangible asset that holds a perceived value for the recipient. There is no expectation that the giver will receive anything in return.

For example, "I gave at the office" has become a dismissive phrase meaning "I already threw money (away) at that cause or issue." In the retail business, we often refer to "giveaways," incidentals.

With giving, the specific donation is often forgotten soon after—by both parties, the giver and the recipient.

Examples of "giving" include the change tossed in the donation can at the grocery store checkout, the check sent in response to a direct mail request by a local organization, or the weekly contribution dropped in the basket passed at church. In each case, there is an implied agreement that the money will be applied in a way most useful or beneficial to the recipient—*specific* usage is not keenly important.

Charity

"Charity," as its Greek and Latin roots suggest, is a gift given out of love. In "charity," there is an implied empathetic or emotional relationship, however brief, between the donor and the beneficiary. Most often, an act of charity is an acknowledgment of need or pain on the recipient's part.

As with "giving," there is no expectation of an exchange, or a return of some tangible sort, to the benefactor initiating an act of charity. The "good feeling," and faith that the pain or need will be diminished to some degree, is considered reward enough.

An act of charity, however, implies an inequality. There is an underlying understanding that the benefactor is the "have" and the beneficiary is the "have not." The relative social (and moral?) inequality of the two parties is unmistakably implied. That is why the notion of "charity" is almost considered a bit too "Dickensian," a touch politically incorrect, by today's standards.

Philanthropy

"Philanthropy" is a notion and act quite apart from "giving" or "charity." The word's Greek and Latin roots attest to the notion that philanthropy is motivated by a deep and abiding love of humanity. In its truest meaning, "philanthropy" implies a deeply felt conviction for the worth of all humanity.

The most effective acts of philanthropy are rooted in the belief that all men and women are truly equals, therefore deserving of the basic essentials of human existence or experience.

Although each philanthropist may define those essentials differently—e.g., a clean environment, sufficient food, exposure to art, safe and adequate housing, a basic education, the freedoms of speech and religion, good health—there is among all philanthropists a unifying respect for the human community.

And, unlike "giving" or "charity," philanthropy demands response. *Philanthropy is a calculated investment made with the expectation that humankind—or some small part of it—will be profoundly, measurably, and permanently changed for the better as a direct result of the contribution.*

Clearly then, "philanthropy" requires vision, a specific notion of the world, or some small subset of it, as a better place. The importance of vision in philanthropy cannot be overemphasized.

"Philanthropy" demands patience and the knowledge that great change rarely happens in a hurry.

And effective philanthropy can become engaged only within the context of a plan, a roadmap for achieving or arriving at the vision.

It is not the dollar amount of the "gift" that separates a donor from a true philanthropist. It is intent, expectation, and vision that separates the two ... not unlike the distinction between someone who "dabbles" in the market and a serious investor.

Part Two

Defining Your Philanthropic Goals

Chapter 2

Drawing on Your Personal History

*In the quiet hours when we are alone
and there is nobody to tell us what fine fellows we are,
we come sometimes upon a moment in which we wonder,
not how much money we are earning,
nor how famous we have become,
but what good we are doing.*

—A.A. Milne

hen a group of philanthropists was recently asked to share their most satisfying giving experiences, virtually none of the answers made reference to a financial contribution to a charity.

One elegant and well-humored lady known for her many generous contributions to charity wistfully recalled a special experience from her early childhood. She remembered the special pleasure she felt whenever her mother would handmake a dress for her. It so happened that her closest school chum was an orphan who lived under much less fortunate circumstances. The young girl asked her mother if she would make a special dress for her friend, offering to forgo a new outfit for herself if her mom would agree. She has never forgotten the experience of sharing that surprise with her friend.

Sadly, it seems that many high-net-worth individuals and families find themselves feeling socially obliged to "share the wealth," but have lost—or perhaps never experienced—a deep satisfaction, enjoyment, delight, or sense of accomplishment in the act of giving. Noblesse oblige has become, for many, a burden disguised as charity.

A number of myths have sprung up around the "joy" of giving:

- **Myth 1:** There is a correlation between the amount of money an individual contributes to charity and the degree of satisfaction experienced in the giving.
- **Myth 2:** The kind and quality of gift recognition influences the donor's satisfaction in making the donation.
- **Myth 3:** There is a greater pleasure in giving as one gets older, or as one becomes financially capable of making ever-larger gifts.

As much as they may deny it, nonprofit organizations solicit contributions based on the assumptions that these myths are true. Yet in surveying individuals and families involved in charitable giving, the truth lies far from the myth.

The story of the woman who recalled the joy of sharing a new dress with her friend is not atypical of the experiences many philanthropists point to as their most gratifying. Most often, their greatest satisfaction came from a small act of kindness that stemmed from the heart, and was received—with overwhelming gratitude and innocence—by an unsuspecting recipient.

Another source of immense pleasure for donors is the gift that repays a small act of kindness that was deeply cherished by the now-philanthropist.

For example, young John Brooks Fuqua had an imagination and curiosity that couldn't be satisfied on the farm where he grew up. He wrote numerous letters to every library in the region asking if he might be allowed to check out books by mail. Only one library reached out to fill the young boy's hunger to read. Many,

many decades later, multimillionaire philanthropist Fuqua repaid that small kindness with gifts totaling $37 million to Duke University—for it was the school's librarian who had responded to the young boy's plea.

Those donors who experience the highest degree of profound or long-lasting satisfaction in giving share a common approach to philanthropy: they are proactive in targeting beneficiaries, rather than reactive.

Most have consciously or unconsciously reviewed their own life experiences to uncover those moments or incidents that most dramatically altered the very course of their life. The incident, act, or experience may have been a very positive one or perhaps a very painful one. But it is one moment that has never been forgotten.

The most satisfied philanthropists seek out individuals and organizations who are passionately and honestly working to bring the possibility of that experience—or the elimination of that experience—to others.

And if no one else is out there "doing it," the philanthropist will often create and fund his or her own initiative to enhance or protect the lives of others.

The philanthropist's experience of giving differs from that of the person who simply "donates." That difference is not unlike the difference in pleasure experienced by a craftsman who has hand-built his chair versus the shopper who picked one up at a department store.

Wealth and Philanthropy

We spoke in the opening of this book about the myth that giving large sums of money makes one a philanthropist. Is there any correlation, then, between wealth and philanthropy? Indirectly, yes.

It is no accident that some of the most effective philanthropists are men and women who succeeded in business. The fruit of that success happens to be money.

The source, and engine, for that success, however, was vision. Very few individuals have become successful in a business, trade, or profession without a vision, a plan for achieving that vision, and the commitment to make that vision a reality. The status quo is never enough for these individuals.

Philanthropy, in its essence, requires vision—a vision of the world as a better place for the human community.

Those who have the vision to succeed in business are also the ones that reap its rewards—wealth. When those same individuals turn their attention and their heart toward the vision of a better world, they have greater financial means than most to apply toward making that social vision a reality.

To put it more simply, the very attributes that made many philanthropists wealthy—vision and drive—are the same attributes that make these individuals "philanthropists," as opposed to just "donors."

These are, to a great degree, individuals who have never disconnected from their roots. They understand from experience that great things can be made to happen if you can, first, conceive of them and, second, focus your resources single-mindedly to making them happen.

This then is the link between wealth and philanthropy: vision.

Women and Philanthropy

A great deal has been written recently about the differences in charitable giving patterns between men and women. A great deal has been speculated about why women seem to contribute less generously than men, why they take longer to make a giving decision, and why they seem to spread their charitable contributions rather than concentrating them.

Where are the female Carnegies, Annenbergs, Soros, Gates, and Turners? Why do women buy the $10,000 gala tables while men endow the $1,000,000 chairs?

Socially, some reasons are quite obvious. First, women have, over the ages, had less independent capital to contribute. Secondly, until only the last generation or three, women have had limited control or input with respect to the family finances. And thirdly, as Gloria Steinem herself admitted, many women share the fear of becoming destitute or homeless—"bag ladies"—in their later years.

Quite simply, women have had neither the means nor motive to play a major role in philanthropy.

But there is another, less apparent but more compelling, reason why women do not wear the mantle of philanthropy comfortably.

Success in business requires vision. Entrepreneurship requires vision. "Practice makes perfect," the saying goes. Men—through business—have had the opportunity to assimilate—and exercise—the most essential attribute required by philanthropy: vision.

The business world is only now truly beginning to welcome women into the ranks of leadership and ownership. Until recently, women have simply not been in a position in society where "vision" was required, or even encouraged as an important attribute. "Vision" has been an underdeveloped talent for women of earlier generations.

Most women are only now, in the post-Eisenhower era, starting to look beyond home, the family, or a job promotion to "envision" a wealth of life, career, and business possibilities.

With respect to business, more and more women are experimenting with and succeeding at entrepreneurship. They are gaining experience in conceiving, working toward, and achieving a long-term vision in the economic arena.

That experience—and the resultant financial wealth—is finally positioning women to play a far more significant role in the philanthropic community.

Again, wealth—a woman's independent wealth—and philanthropy are linked through vision.

Finding a Root for Your Philanthropy

ॐ

To give away money is an easy matter and in any man's power. But to decide to whom to give it, and how large, and when, and for what purpose and how, is neither in every man's power nor an easy matter.

—*Aristotle*

ॐ

So where do you begin your philanthropic journey? Begin with what you know—yourself. Take from the story you know best—the story of your life. In the moments of your life you will find that which has universal meaning: the experiences of love, pain, joy, discovery, loss, wonder, hardship, injustice, faith, triumph.

Recalling those moments isn't easy. Like watercolors, thirty, forty, seventy years start to "run" together, and those brilliant life-altering moments get lost in the great "wash" of time.

How do you re-discover them? Three roads are offered here to help lead you to the defining experiences of your life. Recalling those experiences can inspire and guide your philanthropy in directions you have never considered. Yet these may be the areas in which you will experience your greatest philanthropic satisfaction.

❦

It is by spending ONESELF that one becomes rich.
—*Sarah Bernhardt*

❦

Exercise 1: Simply Answer the Questions—Simply

The answers to these questions are not in themselves intended to lead you directly to a personal philanthropic focus. Rather, they are designed to take you down some of the main roads of your personal history. Roads where you might just stumble upon a long-unexplored moment that altered—or could have altered—your life. Linger a moment and you just might discover that which inspires you to change the world. That is where to plant the root of your philanthropy.

By the way, don't waste this wonderful opportunity to share your story with someone older or younger who is special to you. Fix a cup of tea or coffee (or gin), turn down the phone, and share those key memories with someone who matters. They'll love really "seeing" you, and in opening your story up to others, you will be amazed at how many long-forgotten details re-emerge. You also might consider taping your reminiscences—your oral history can prove a rich resource later as you broaden your philanthropic horizons (and your family will treasure having this valuable keepsake).

Childhood Experiences

1. What are the four most specific moments you remember?
2. What were your three most positive experiences?
3. Which were the three most painful?
4. Where was your favorite place to go alone?

Adolescence

1. What were the biggest challenges and rewards of your adolescence:
   - At home?
   - At school?
   - With friends?
   - With the opposite sex?
2. Where was your favorite place to go alone as an adolescent?
3. Where was your favorite place to go with others?
4. With what adult outside your family did you spend the most amount of time?
5. Who was your favorite relative?
6. Who was your least favorite relative?

Young Adulthood

1. When was the exact moment that you first felt that you were an adult?
2. What were the circumstances of that flash of self-awareness?
3. What were your goals and dreams at 21?
4. What boosted you to reach those goals?
5. What blocked you from trying to achieve your dreams?

Adulthood

1. At 35, what was your favorite place to go to alone?
2. What was your favorite place to go to with the important people in your life?

3. What periods of your life brought you the greatest stress or anger?
4. What experiences inspired your greatest joy or insight?
5. What significant crises or losses have you faced?
6. What was the single greatest surprise of your life?

Exploring the World

1. What three life experiences most altered your world view?
2. Describe your first experience in a foreign country.
3. What amazed you?
4. What saddened you?
5. What would draw you back there?
6. What would keep you from returning?

Key People in Your Life

1. Who were the individuals who stopped to really get to know you?
2. Who passed you by when you needed them most?
3. Who was the first person of another race that you met?
4. Who was the first person from another country that you met?
5. Who was the first person of another faith that you met?
6. What were these people like?

Exercise 2:
They Could Write a Book About My Life

You have been approached by an author who would like to write the story of your life, the definitive biography.

You agree—on one condition. You will provide the title for each chapter, and you will write the opening and closing paragraphs for each one as well.

The author enthusiastically accepts your condition, and tells you that each chapter will cover ten years of your life, starting with your birth. You have one week to bring him the chapter titles, and the first and last paragraphs for each ten-year section.

Begin to write.

Exercise 3:
Do as I Do ...
Or, Find a Philanthropic Role Model

Many years ago, a wise man was teaching his daughter to swim. Stroke, kick, breathe, stroke, kick, breathe. She couldn't get the knack of it despite her father's coaching. It was too much to concentrate on at one time. Her legs and her arms seemed to want fight each other, and sputtering the horrible chlorinated water was the closest she could come to breathing rhythmically.

The father, realizing that the child would never learn to enjoy swimming this way, called her out of the water.

Pointing to a young woman gracefully stroking laps in the pool, he urged his daughter to just jump in the pool and "pretend you're her." She did just that, and ever since, she too has been a graceful and confident swimmer.

May these stories of philanthropists both anonymous and renowned inspire you to just jump in...

- Few know the story of Andrew Carnegie's passion for building libraries. As a boy in Pittsburgh, he and his brother spent hours with other working kids enjoying the 400-volume private library of a Colonel Anderson. When Carnegie grew wealthy, he never forgot what he termed the Colonel's "precious generosity" and committed his resources to establishing a network of free libraries across the nation that continue to stand today as one of the single greatest philanthropic undertakings of all time.

- Zachary Fisher, 86, was awarded the Medal of Freedom, the country's highest civilian honor. As a young construction worker in the late 1930s, he suffered a knee injury that disqualified him from service during World War II. He was devastated when he was refused induction in 1942 and never forgot the price that others paid to defend his freedom and that of the nation. He went on to become a successful developer. He has used his wealth to support the families of soldiers killed in the service of the country. In 1983, he sent a check for $10,000 to the children of each of the 241 Marines and service personnel killed in the bombing of a Beirut barracks, to help pay for their college education. In 1989, Fisher sent $25,000 to the family of each man lost in the turret explosion aboard the battleship Iowa. He has sent another 600 checks of at least $10,000 to the families of other military personnel killed while serving. "I always felt that I owed something to the men and women who defended my freedom and allowed me to become so successful in such a great country."

- Joan Kroc, widow of McDonald's magnate Ray Kroc, is legendary for her generosity to charities and victims of disaster across the U.S. Her $80 million gift to the Salvation Army, however, was inspired by one of her fondest memories of her late husband—he would dress as Santa, ringing a bell for Salvation Army donations.

- Osceola McCarty, an 88-year-old laundress, gave her life savings of $150,000 to finance scholarships at a local Mississippi college. She had never enjoyed the luxury of an education.

- Famous talent agent Michael Ovitz repaid UCLA Medical Center for providing medicine for his child in the middle of the night with a gift of $25 million in Disney stock.

- Robert E. McDonough, founder of RemedyTemp, Inc., honored Georgetown University, his alma mater, with a $30 million multi-year contribution. McDonough believes the night-school education he got at Georgetown while working Capital Hill as a policeman in the 1940s laid the foundation for his later success in business.

- Far less dramatic experiences can also inspire philanthropic gifts. The memory of Maddie, his late schnauzer, was the inspiration for David Dufflefield, the founder, president, and CEO of PeopleSoft Inc., to establish a $200 million fund for animal welfare organizations. The basis for his philanthropic passion: honoring Maddie, who was always there for him with "unconditional love" during the periods of greatest personal and professional stress.

Summary

It's not impossible to regain the pleasure of giving. All it requires is searching your own life experiences to find those that touched your soul. Then seek out individuals and groups who are passionately and honestly working to bring the possibility of that experience to others. Your hands, your heart, your laughter or tears engaged in that endeavor will bring you the joy of giving. Do what you love, then let the money follow.

Note: **See Appendix A: General Fields of Nonprofit Endeavor** for more information on arcas you might be interested in.

Chapter 3

Selecting a "Sphere of Influence" for Your Philanthropy

❦

Apart from the ballot box,
philanthropy presents the one opportunity the individual has
to express his meaningful choice over
the direction in which our society will progress.

—George Kirstein

❦

ow that you have identified or narrowed the field of need or service in which you would like to provide support, your next mission will be to identify the "sphere of influence" within which you wish your philanthropy to have an impact.

Think of the "sphere of influence" as the circle or segment of society within which you can make a difference through your philanthropy. A good analogy for illustrating the concept of sphere of influence is our governmental structure.

A mayor's sphere of influence is his city, a governor's is her state. The president's circle of responsibility is the nation. The secretary-general of the United Nations has within his sphere of influence much of the globe.

Within government, the larger your sphere of influence, to some degree, the more dilute is your power to have a profound impact within that circle. Unless, of course, you have a strong base of support and enormous resources.

The same is true in philanthropy. To make change—even constructive change—in society, the greater your resources and number of like-minded supporters, the more likely you will be to succeed.

The philanthropist's decision with respect to his or her chosen sphere of influence is a critical one. It is a decision that will be predicated in part upon:

- The choice of field(s) drawing the donor's passionate interest
- The size of investment the donor wishes to make
- How quickly the donor wishes to see a return on his or her investment

There are essentially four spheres of influence to choose from as a charitable donor. Within each, there may be sub-categories, and there is a great deal of overlap between these spheres, but the general circles of influence can be distinguished as follows:

- Personal or individual
- Community
- Institutional or infrastructural
- Policy

How does selection of a sphere of influence guide your charitable giving activities? Let's look at an example.

Making Changes in the World Through Education

One small family foundation in a desert community of Southern California determined that academic opportunity had provided the key to success that led their family to prosperity. They decided to share their good fortune by making scholarships available to promising, low-income students in the family's hometown. Each year, they pay partial or full tuition for a group of students who otherwise would not have the resources necessary to attend college, graduate school, professional school, or a vocational institute. This family elected to engage their philanthropy at a very *personal* level, impacting individual lives as their method for changing the world.

Similarly, in 1997, philanthropists John Walton and Ted Forstmann donated $6 million to fund one thousand scholarships for low-income Washington, D.C. children to attend the private schools of their choice.

A donor in another part of the country elected to make his impact on a *community* level. This individual chose to contribute $10,000 to an educational foundation benefiting all of the schools in a particular community. Although he could not trace the impact of his gift on a specific child—or even a specific school—he believed that the application of his resources would create an improved school environment for all students in that community.

In perhaps the most famous contemporary gift dedicated to impacting *infrastructure*, former U.S. ambassador and renowned philanthropist Walter Annenberg donated $500 million for the restructuring and reform of public schools in the U.S. By applying resources to redesign the school systems in key cities, new models for public school administration and education would be developed that could be applied to public schools throughout the country.

And, illustrating the fourth option for a sphere of influence, numerous private foundations engage in support of policy research institutes and "think tanks" seeking methods by which our educational system can be improved through altering or amending legislation or public *policy*.

How do you determine which "sphere of influence" is right for your philanthropic giving?" To a great degree, that will be determined by how important it is for you to see the impact of your giving. Do you expect to see a measurable change in a life or improvement in society within your lifetime?

Impacting Individual Lives

By selecting to assist individuals as your sphere of influence, you would be choosing to use your charitable giving to immediately impact one or more person's lives. The impact on their quality of life may be permanent, temporary, or even momentary. Some examples:

- Scholarship aid
- Contributions of money or goods to food banks or homeless shelters
- Grants to individual visual or performing artists to encourage their work
- Donations to agencies offering support to elderly or sick individuals
- Underwriting delivery of pharmaceutical drugs or medical supplies to disaster-stricken or impoverished areas
- Funding the purchase of teddy bears for toddlers involved in domestic violence or abuse
- Making someone's "dying wish" come true
- Underwriting the telephone costs for a rape crisis or suicide hotline
- Purchasing bicycles for individuals in rural communities
- Donating books and supplies to a local adult litcracy or vocational training program
- Subsidizing veterinary service costs for low-income families or older adults
- Sponsoring a mentoring program
- Gifting to hands-on human service agencies such as the Red Cross or the Salvation Army

The list of possible ways in which your philanthropy could directly—and measurably—touch and change individual lives is virtually endless. And such acts of generosity do not have to be restricted to your home community or even to the continent on which you reside.

Impacting a Community

In a "community-focused" approach to philanthropy, the donor desires to use his or her charitable giving in order to improve the overall quality of life among a defined group of people. The community may be defined by geographic area, ethnic or racial heritage, age group, gender, or some other common attribute. Support is generally provided to an organization or agency already organized to serve the needs of that community. For instance:

- Supporting a locally based cultural or natural history center
- Giving to a synagogue, church, mosque, meeting hall, or faith-affiliated school
- Contributing to a senior citizens service agency
- Donating for a community park, playground, or youth activity center
- Subsidizing an ethnic dance or music group
- Underwriting construction of a cancer, AIDS, or emergency illness clinic
- Endowing a library foundation

In community-focused giving, it is often possible to trace the benefit or impact of the gift on individual lives, even though there is a strongly social aspect to the impetus for the gift.

Impacting an Institution or Infrastructure

Focusing giving on an institution provides the philanthropist with the opportunity to have a profound impact on the life of a particular or unique institution, such as a:

- School
- Hospital
- Museum
- Zoo
- Nature conservancy

The underlying philosophy in selecting this sphere of influence is that, by improving or strengthening a key or core institution, a number of lives will be improved or enhanced, although perhaps no one specific life will be improved in some measurable fashion.

We see this on a larger scale where philanthropists have supported nonprofit or non-governmental agencies, efforts, and social movements that have sought to reform or re-form "institutions" or infrastructures that they believe to be fundamentally flawed, immoral, or inhumane, for example:

- UNICEF
- CIVICUS
- Amnesty International
- Greenpeace
- International Campaign to Ban Landmines
- Physicians for Human Rights

Impacting Policy

Philanthropists involved in this sphere of influence support efforts that examine and encourage alternative approaches to complex social issues, particularly those that have their roots in the law, regulation, politics, or "codified" social custom. Donors seek to encourage social, legal, or economic reform through research and lawful systems change. Common targets:

- Discrimination on the basis of race, sex, creed, color, or sexual orientation as it applies to housing, employment, or education
- Abrogation of basic human rights such as freedom of speech or religion, or the freedom to congregate
- Denial of legal rights guaranteed under the Constitution
- Medical care reform

Weighing the Benefits of Each "Sphere of Influence"

For those philanthropists wishing to see the fastest and perhaps most dramatic results from their giving, the individual sphere of influence is the most likely to provide the greatest level of satisfaction.

Benefiting an Individual

For example, providing tuition for a student who otherwise might not be in school allows you as the donor to know exactly how and for whom your money will be used. If you have done your "due diligence" before making the gift, you can be fairly certain that your contribution will have a profound, serious, and lasting impact on the life of that individual.

You will also be able to track whether that investment provided a worthwhile, measurable philanthropic return: Did the child stay in school? How was their academic performance? Did they become someone who could contribute to the world in a way they otherwise might not have? Did they move into employment or a profession that would not have been an option without education? Did they go on to inspire, assist, or nurture the educational aspirations of others?

Philanthropy, the "love for all humanity," is rooted in a vision for the world, a long-term vision. Philanthropy, therefore, invests for the long term. By engaging as a donor within an individual-centered sphere of influence, you are sowing seeds for tomorrow.

In other words, the student given an otherwise unattainable educational opportunity today—in a classroom, or at home, or in the community—will enjoy the benefits of that opportunity not just today, but at that point in the future when today's opportunities will be seen as having been the building blocks for the future he or she has attained.

Even more simply, by positively impacting a child today, you create the possibility of a better world for all of us tomorrow.

Strengthening a Community

Focusing your philanthropy on a community-centered sphere of influence has some of the benefits of directly affecting individuals, while also providing for slow, measured, recognizable improvement in the overall quality of life of a community.

Leo Adler, a multi-millionaire magazine distributor, got his start selling papers on the streets of Baker City, Oregon at the age of 9. He never moved away from the home where he was raised by his immigrant parents. When he passed away at age 98, he left an unexpected $20 million to Baker City and its 10,000 residents. From the Little League, to the library, to the local fire department, there does not seem to be an area of community life that Adler's largesse has not touched. In addition, the foundation he left behind makes scholarships available to every graduate of the town's two high schools, as well as to residents seeking higher degrees or professional training. His philanthropy will have a profound effect on the entire community of Baker for generations to come.

Some philanthropists choose to benefit an entire community for somewhat "selfish" reasons (although, as we've pointed out, "philanthropy" by definition is an unselfish endeavor). They select the community where family, loved ones, or others of great personal significance or importance to them have established their home. By improving the life of the community as a whole, these philanthropists know that their family members will enjoy the benefits as well.

This holds true for a corporate "family" as well. PepsiCo's chief executive officer, Roger Enrico added his 1998 salary (save $1) to the company's $1 million scholarship fund for the children of company employees earning less than $60,000 per year. Enrico regularly refers to these loyal employees as the company's "front line" and felt he and PepsiCo should invest their philanthropic funds where their company's "community" could benefit.

There is one additional benefit to engaging in community-focused philanthropy—whatever the make-up or definition of your selected "community": The more people individually touched by your philanthropy, the greater the legacy you leave. Just ask the people of Baker City, Oregon, or the children of PepsiCo's employees.

Targeting an Institution

Institutionally focused philanthropy is, frankly, very closely related to community-oriented philanthropy: the institution and its beneficiaries are, in a sense, the target community. Depending on the fashion in which the donor chooses to support the institution, the impact can be immediate and visible, or it can be somewhat more subtle and less apparent to the public eye.

For example, the philanthropist choosing an institutional sphere of influence might elect to provide the capital funding for a new wing, or to establish an endowment to ensure the long-term viability of an important new program or service. The results of such a gift could be visible very quickly.

On the other hand, the philanthropist might choose to provide funding for critical operating expenses needed by a battered women's shelter. The benefits of such gifts are rarely visible to the general public, or even to the donors themselves. Yet without general operating and overhead funds (which will be discussed in detail in Chapter 6), most institutions—in fact, most charitable organizations—could not exist to do their work.

Tackling Infrastructure

The effort to effect a change in infrastructure is among the most daunting challenges that a philanthropist will ever face. Ambassador Annenberg's unprecedented gift to improve the public education system in our nation is the most visible undertaking of philanthropy in the area of systems change that this country has seen.

If one were to examine whether this sizable investment has had an impact on public education, however, one could not look to an individual school, or even a school system, to determine whether it has had an impact. It will be many years before it can be determined whether this was a successful investment. It will take the efforts of many other philanthropists and activists to monitor, evaluate, and promote what has been learned or experienced through the application of the original gift. And even more time will pass before all of these gains are promulgated and replicated throughout our public education system nationally.

The philanthropist embarking on a journey to transform infrastructure must have patience and be willing to accept that the impact of his or her contribution may not be apparent until long after the gift is made. This can be very frustrating for many newer philanthropists, just as it is for newcomers to the stock market. Frankly, most of us would like immediate proof that our investment is working.

Impacting Policy

Devoting charitable funds to a policy-centered sphere of influence is among the most important, expensive, and long-term investments that a philanthropist may choose to make. In the policy arena, the philanthropist also has the least amount of control over the outcome of his or her investment. That is, constructive research may not, ultimately, result in a policy change.

The Size of Your Stake

How much money you have to invest will also play a role in selecting your sphere of influence. Practically speaking, it is far less expensive to pay a child's tuition than it is to restructure the American educational system. It is cheaper to fund a volunteer-run literacy program than to build a library. It costs less to provide meals to the home-bound on holidays than to reform the agricultural economy of a third-world nation. It is more economical to pay for one man's lung surgery than to fund a cure for cancer.

Establishing a Legacy

Lastly, you can use the "By whom do I want to be remembered?" test to help determine which sphere of influence will be most satisfying to you.

For example, would you like to be remembered and honored by an individual or individuals who for many years to come will gratefully acknowledge that they would not have had the opportunities they were given without your generosity? If this is the legacy you wish to leave, then the individual sphere of influence would probably be most satisfying to you.

If it would mean more to you to have your name linked to a specific institution with which you had an important or significant relationship, or if you would like your legacy to be tied (inexorably!) with the future of that institution, then the institutional sphere of influence will be more attractive to you as a philanthropist.

Of course, you may wish later that your philanthropy had taken another form. Famed showman P.T. Barnum was a benefactor of Tufts University. When Jumbo, Barnum's famed circus elephant, died, it was stuffed and enshrined at Tufts. The memorial "trophy" was destroyed in a fire, but was later re-created in bronze and ensconced in Barnum Hall. As might be expected, both Barnum and Jumbo have been the objects of much humor around that campus over the years. On second thought, that may be just the legacy the great entertainer *intended* to leave behind!

If you would like to be remembered by a town or community of people that holds a special place for you, then community-focused giving would be most suited to your style of philanthropy.

Lastly, except in rare instances will any one individual or foundation be remembered for or credited with spearheading a substantive social or policy change. The collaborative nature of such work and the timeframe required for success in achieving social change do not fit well with singular attribution. If name recognition is important to you, the policy sphere of influence may not feel very rewarding.

Summary

It is now time to answer this important question: relative to your charitable financial resources, the form you wish your legacy to take, and the immediacy with which you wish to witness the results of your philanthropy, which sphere of influence is right for you?

Your careful consideration of this matter can help you achieve a greater personal satisfaction from your philanthropic investments.

Chapter 4

Where Will You Make Your Mark?

*The money was made in New York,
so I've given it back to New York.*
—Brooke Astor

ne of the most exciting choices that a philanthropist will make is the geographic region or area where he or she will make that philanthropic investment. And there are many reasons why one might choose a particular area over another.

Television icon Johnny Carson, for example, donated $150,000 to the community center in Logan, Iowa, the town where his grandparents lived. As a child growing up in Nebraska, Carson would visit his grandfather, C.N. ("Kit") Carson, who was mayor of Logan from 1944 to 1948.

The obvious choice would be to make the charitable investment in an area or region close to the donor's main residence. By investing close to home, the philanthropist may find it easier to monitor and assess the effectiveness of his or her charitable contribution.

However, there may be other factors that prospective donors will want to consider before limiting themselves to "the neighborhood."

When Size DOES Matter

For example, a charitable investment in a small town is more likely to have a measurable impact than the same-sized contribution made in a large city.

Or, if one of your motivations as a philanthropist is public recognition, the level of your gift may have a far higher value in a smaller town or community than it would in a major metropolitan area.

There are other benefits, however, to making your philanthropic investment in a large city. For example, there seems to be a trend for urban challenges, problems, and opportunities to resonate out from the urban centers to suburban and outlying metropolitan areas, and ultimately to rural areas. That same pattern, to some degree, can be reflected in the effects of charitable giving. In other words, by successfully addressing a social issue or challenge in a metropolitan setting, the philanthropist may create a model or paradigm that will translate to outlying areas as well.

Regional Considerations

Some philanthropists may elect to benefit a region rather than a specific city or town. For example, some may choose a remote, mountainous, or desert area for their philanthropic base, recognizing that organizations in isolated areas have a much harder time attracting philanthropic support than agencies based in metropolitan or major industrial areas.

The fact is, the economic realities of an area with no major corporate or industrial presence, and which is populated by families living at or below the poverty level, will have a very difficult time attracting major gifts or strong corporate support for its nonprofit community. Yet the social issues and challenges in an isolated region—issues of literacy, hunger, educational opportunity, health, nutrition, and environmental hazards, to name a few—may be far more critical than those same or similar challenges in an urban setting.

Trying to benefit an entire state may be, understandably, difficult. Size and population are just two factors to consider. As you might imagine, it would be more reasonable (and less costly) to attempt to have an impact on the entire state of, say, Rhode Island, than to strive to have a comparable impact on the state of California.

Choosing a state focus for your philanthropy, however, is not without some strong merits. The fact is, there are some states that are more acutely suffering the key social and economic challenges plaguing our nation today than others, for example crime, poverty, unemployment, illitcracy, and discrimination. In states that are making a concerted effort to address those challenges, the climate for a public/private philanthropic partnership might be especially conducive or welcoming to interested charitable donors. Another strategic approach to funding might be to weave a statc-wide "safety net" linking agencies serving similar client populations.

It's a Small, Small World

With advances in telecommunications, travel, and technology, the world is becoming a smaller and smaller place. Social and economic factors in one nation are no longer confined within its borders. Social change, social advances, and social challenges—not unlike political and economic influences—today spread quickly across the globe.

Just as a failing economy in Russia influences the market economies of the rest of the globe, just as political challenges in China pose political challenges for nations around the world, philanthropic investments in one country or another can have a profound effect beyond the borders of that one nation.

Consequently many philanthropists are looking beyond ethnic allegiances and national borders to identify critical areas or regions in the world where their charitable investment can provoke constructive change, not only in that community, but in other communities strategically linked to that base. For example, by providing philanthropic assistance to countries south of the United States, it might be possible to ease social and employment challenges within U.S. border communities where immigration has become a major social factor. For other examples of international giving, one need look no further than the geographic choices of George Soros and Ted Turner in order to see how philanthropy can incite "the domino effect."

Big Fish, Small Pond

In selecting a home base, a philanthropist should not ignore the desire to be recognized or acknowledged for his or her generosity. For that reason, should you choose to make your gifts in a small town or perhaps a rural area, you will probably establish a more visible legacy than if you invested that same dollar amount of support in a major metropolitan area. Think about whether it would be more satisfying for you to be "a big fish in a small pond" or the opposite. Put another way, in all candor, how big of a "splash" would you like your gift to make?

For example, Charles and Peggy Pearce of Corsicana, Texas, donated their important collection of contemporary Western art to tiny Navarro College in Corsicana. Pearce, a Cornell University alumnus, decided not to contribute the artwork to his alma mater, as he felt the collection would not be as important to the prestigious university as it would be to Navarro.

Reaping What You Sow

Another consideration in establishing or selecting a home base for your philanthropy is the whole question of whether you wish to "concentrate" your charitable investment in one area for the purpose of exacting the maximum effect for your money, or whether to "sprinkle" your giving in a variety of community settings and geographic areas in order to "seed" change across a broader base.

Making Your Decision

All of the above factors may and should have an influence on your decision when selecting a home base for your philanthropy.

To help you explore just some of your options, below is a list of the most frequently cited locations for philanthropic largesse:

- The town, city, state, region, or country where you were born
- The place where you spent your early childhood
- The location where you attended grammar school
- The community where your high school was located
- The college town of your youth
- The place where you spent family vacations
- The city or town that was your first "home away from home"
- The home of your grandparents, favorite aunt and uncle, or other important people in your life
- The place you fell in love
- The city or town where you were married
- The area most closely identified with your family tree
- The place where you made your fortune, or your philanthropy found its footing
- The neighborhood where your children were born
- The town or city where your grandchildren or great-grandchildren currently live
- The place where you have retired, are planning to retire, or consider your second home
- An area that delighted or moved you on a visit
- A place that you read about, or learned about on television or in a movie
- A location that you have dreamed of visiting one day (here's your chance!)

Putting the "Phun" Back in Philanthropy

One adventurous philanthropic couple decided that it would be great fun to become anonymous angels for an unsuspecting community where they had no prior connection. They selected the beneficiary town by opening an atlas of the United States and, with eyes closed, simply pointing. They then repeated the "search" process using the appropriate state map.

The couple took a short trip to the town to see it for themselves, then began contacting the local community foundation and other umbrella services agencies for more in-depth information on the town's needs. They quietly researched the charities in the area to determine which seemed to be operating most effectively. As they learned about specific programs or services that were having a positive impact on the overall life of the community, they channeled substantial contributions to them.

They kept their secret closely, never revealing their identity to the many charities they endowed. And they delighted in their "sleuthing" almost as much as they did in their philanthropy.

Summary

Choosing a home base for your philanthropy can be great fun and a way to honor, remember, or repay a community or place for the role it plays or played in your life or in the life of someone important to you. Don't let geography or distance limit your options. Chapter 7 will show you how to find worthwhile charities in whatever part of the country or world you choose, without having to stray much further than your telephone or mailbox.

Chapter 5

Risk and Return: Defining Your "Comfort Zone"

❧

The trouble is, if you don't risk anything,
you risk even more.

—Erica Jong

❧

ust as with any other form of financial investment, sound philanthropic investment requires an assessment of one's comfort level with "risk."

Where is the "risk" in philanthropy? It lies in how effectively your contribution will be used by a given organization to accomplish the specific charitable objectives you have set. More specifically, "risk" is determined by how capable an organization is of using your donation to make the greatest possible impact on the area of service that is your focus.

Your charitable contribution to one nonprofit can have more or less risk associated with it based on several factors:

- The organization's stage of development
- The size of the charity
- The nonprofit's budget

· Just as with traditional investing, making your contribution to a "venture" organization—one that is new, young, or initiating a dramatically innovative program—has more inherent risk than donating to a large, well-established, older nonprofit of the "blue chip" variety.

In return for assuming the risk, however, you may gain the ability to have a greater impact with a smaller overall contribution. For example, newer, "venture" nonprofits frequently have lower overhead and tend to expend a higher percentage of their funds on service. The downside is the uncertainty of whether the organization will survive, much less thrive, over the long term. Should it fail, your contribution will have suffered the risk of having had only a momentary effect.

For example, donating $5,000 to a new charity run by volunteers with an annual operating budget of $10,000 can have a substantial impact on their ability to provide services—if those services are well-planned and well-executed. But if the organization goes out of business eighteen months later, will you feel that you made a poor investment?

On the other hand, the "safer" the investment—with an established organization with a track record of service—the more reason you have to believe that your contribution will be used effectively. Further, you can feel fairly secure that your investment will serve as a "building block" atop the charity's already established foundation of success.

Although your investment risk is lower, the immediate impact of your donation may be diminished by the larger scale of operations. That is to say, your $5,000 will have less impact on an operation whose overall program and service budget is $5 million or $25 million than it will on a small, "venture" charity.

Put another way, the "safer" the investment, the more certain you can be that there will be a positive and longer-term return on that investment. However, that return may be incrementally smaller. For example, an organization such as the Red Cross is well-established, and has a well-publicized, successful track record. A donation to the Red Cross may not have as profound an impact in the larger scheme of its overall activities, but you can feel secure (at lower risk) that your contribution will be soundly utilized.

The "Lifecycles" of a Nonprofit

❦

In all things there is a law of cycles.
—Tacitus

❦

Virtually every nonprofit or charitable organization will move through three distinct phases over the course of its lifetime. At each stage of its development, the organization will have unique needs, unique challenges, and unique opportunities. Also at each stage, the nonprofit will pose unique challenges and offer a unique potential for return. By determining an organization's position in its cycle of development, the philanthropic investor can more accurately assess the potential risks and rewards of contributing to that charity. In this chapter, the "lifecycles" of a charitable organization will be examined.

The "Emerging" Stage

The first stage of development is the "emerging" or grass-roots stage. This is that critical one- to two-year phase immediately following the launch of a new charity. This phase is marked by several distinctive characteristics.

Generally, the newly formed organization is headed by its founder, someone with a very strong vision and energy and who will try to make that vision a reality.

The leadership of the organization at this stage generally consists of a relatively small group of like-minded people who subscribe to the founder's mission and vision for the charity.

Unless there has been an unusual infusion of cash by the

founder, most nonprofits at this early stage face daunting financial challenges. In an effort to overcome those challenges, it is critical that the emerging organization establish a solid foundation of supporters who share a commitment to its mission and are willing to back that commitment with a financial investment.

Many organizations in this initial stage are struggling so hard for survival and to "get the message out" that they do not spend the requisite amount of time developing a detailed and actionable strategic plan that will lead the organization through its next several years.

At this stage, the organization presumably has defined or is developing some new and better way of providing a service or program to a population whose need is not being adequately met. *This* is where tremendous opportunity exists for the charitable investor who is seeking to have an impact through support of an innovative initiative.

To get involved with an emerging grass-roots organization can be tremendously gratifying for a donor "getting in on the ground floor" in support of a program or service that might have a profound influence on the community.

The risk in supporting an organization at this stage of development is that the group might not evolve past this stage. It might not develop a strong governing board; a sound leadership and staff; a solid corps of volunteers, clients, or constituents; or, most importantly, the broad base of financial resources necessary to sustain the emerging agency in those first two years.

Philanthropists seeking to support an emerging organization with an innovative program can minimize the risk to their investment and help ensure its long-term return by doing the following:

- Examine the organization's written strategic plan to determine whether it is realistic and reliable, and whether it will lead to achieving the charity's stated vision.
- Carefully study the written program or service outlines to ensure that they make sense and to determine whether a strong ongoing and follow-up evaluation component is built into program activities.

- Review the credentials of the individuals and professionals who established the nonprofit and who designed the program or service that you will support. Do they have the experience and expertise to undertake a new enterprise?
- Determine whether the group is open and eager to draw additional supporters and experts into the ranks. They will have to be successful fundraisers and "friend raisers" if the organization is to thrive.
- In addition to funding the actual program, service, or operating overhead of the organization, insist that a portion of the funds you provide be utilized for leadership training, technical assistance, and fund development training for the key people associated with the charity.
- Lastly, don't walk away from your investment—stay in touch with the organization and its leaders to ensure that they are following the strategic plan and are implementing sound fund development and financial plans for the long-term health of the organization.

Should your charitable gift to an emerging or grass-roots organization pay off, the rewards can be enormous. In addition to providing programs and services in an innovative fashion to a populace in need, you have supported the establishment of a working model that can be replicated in other communities both far and near, thereby multiplying many times over the value of your initial charitable investment.

The Stage of "Maturity"

The second stage of development in the life of a nonprofit can be called the "maturing" stage. This stage is characterized by the following:

- The organization has survived infancy ("the terrible twos") and is getting stronger every day.
- The organization has recognized the need for an expanded, more diverse, more professional, and more knowledgeable board of directors. These individuals understand that they are charged with overseeing the health of the organization at present, as well as charting its course for the future, and for

securing the resources necessary to navigate that course.
- There is now a paid management team, which includes specialists in the administrative functions, as well as experts in program and service areas, who are responsible for the day-to-day operations of the nonprofit.
- The mission and image of the charity are fairly well-established. The emphasis is on ensuring that the organization's message is consistent and highly visible, as opposed to re-crafting it.
- Financially, the mature organization is operating on an even keel, always looking for new supporters and sources of funding, while recognizing the importance of maintaining the allegiance of existing donors.

At this stage of organizational development, the risk to your charitable investment—relative to return—is at its lowest. Programs and services are, theoretically, running smoothly, they have a proven track record, and they are serving an appropriate number of people relative to the size of their annual operating budget.

In fact, it may seem like a "boring" investment. However, in this stage of its development, an organization can find it extremely difficult to secure ongoing support for successful initiatives. It seems like a paradox—when things are going well, it's almost more difficult to find donors who will invest in an ongoing program.

The reason for this is simple. Many charitable investors are always looking for what's new, what's exciting, what's innovative. The ongoing program starts to look like the "meat loaf" course on a buffet of great variety. Therefore, the philanthropist looking to make a very safe investment—one whose return can be fairly well predicted—can accomplish a great deal while risking very little by looking to support an organization that is in this stage of its development.

Where is the risk in a "maintenance"-phase organization? The risk lies in the possibility that the leadership will fall into complacency because things are running so smoothly. With things going well, trustees may become less active in pursuing new supporters. Donations level off as a result. New clients cannot receive services because funding is slipping even as the costs of providing them are rising. Meanwhile, volunteers, donors, and the community at large are looking for the next exciting program coming down the pike.

The biggest risk to the philanthropist donating to a maturing organization arises when the charity fails to assess or acknowledge changes in the environment in which it serves. Such changes might include a shifting demographic (e.g., the ethnic or cultural mix in the community), upturns or downturns in the economy, a change in the funding stream, advances in the organization's field of service (e.g., breakthroughs in medical research), or encouraging results from new or more innovative methodologies.

Another way to explain the notion of "changes in the environment" is by illustration. The eradication of polio was a dramatic alteration to the environment in which the March of Dimes came into existence. The March of Dimes shifted its focus in order to accommodate the changed medical research and support needs of that time.

A more contemporary example is the changing environment in which AIDS-focused charities function. Not many years ago, the mission of direct service organizations was to provide support for a dying constituency and their loved ones. With the advances in AIDS treatment, service organizations are now shifting their focus to providing assistance with the care and management of individuals who can and will live for many years despite carrying the AIDS virus. Thus, a significant shift in the medical treatment of AIDS required charities that focus in that area to adjust both mission and programming in order to stay responsive to the changed needs of their service population. With the advances in AIDS treatment, however, came a change in the public's perception of the seriousness of the epidemic. In some communities, that change in perception has negatively affected funding for AIDS-focused charities.

Effective organizations in the field of AIDS-related services have had to remain flexible and responsive to these "changes in the environment" in order to remain both financially and functionally viable.

Philanthropists contributing to a mature organization can insure their investment by insisting on and supporting ongoing professional development on the part of the organization's leadership—board and staff—as well as encouraging and funding access to information that may have a bearing on the future course of the organization.

The biggest concern for you as a donor supporting an organization at this stage of development should be that the good work being accomplished as a result of your contribution will cease when your funding ceases; the organization's leadership has not planned nor made provisions for its future funding stream.

Ask to see the charity's strategic plan as a means of assessing its preparedness for the future.

The "Renewal/Revitalization" Stage

The third significant stage in the life of a charitable organization is the phase of renewal or revitalization. This is the stage through which the organization transforms itself in response to environmental factors (or market forces) to ensure that it continues to be as responsive as possible to the needs of its service population.

Typical of this stage:

- The organization is undergoing a substantial degree of change: its programs and services are being updated, revamped, or in some cases perhaps eliminated.
- New programs and services are being developed and implemented to meet the changing needs of the service population.
- The mission of the organization may change somewhat to more accurately reflect the agency's response to the changing needs of the service population.
- The organization is undertaking a revitalized effort to establish its image, its visibility, and its mission before the community in order to attract volunteers from segments of the community that have not yet been tapped, to attract clients for its programs and services, and most important, to attract new and expanded funding sources.

In some fashion, this stage of an organization's development is not completely unlike the emerging or grass-roots stage in that it is marked by intense innovation and a moderate to high degree of organizational risk.

This, too, is an extremely exciting time for the philanthropic investor to get involved with an organization. On the one hand, the organization has been in existence for some period of years, thereby ensuring that the charitable investment is not a totally risky one.

On the other hand, it is an opportunity for the philanthropic investor to get involved in innovative programs and services leading to new solutions, and to participate in the revitalization of the charity's mission.

To ensure your charitable investment at this phase of an organization's development, you should encourage the charity to engage in safe and sound risk, as well as productive change. At the same time, be sure that the charity is not simply engaging in change for the sake of change. In other words, you should keep a close eye on the motives underlying a changing dynamic within an organization or program. If innovation is the result of a clear assessment of alterations in the environment, this will bode well for the organization. If, however, dramatic change is an impulsive act meant to "shock" the organization out of a slump, you would do well to withhold financial support at this time.

Starting All Over Again

❦

Force never moves in a straight line,
but always in a curve vast as the universe,
and therefore eventually returns whence it issued forth,
but upon a higher arc,
for the universe has progressed since it started.
—*The Kabbalah*

❦

An organization that has successfully navigated the stage of renewal or revitalization in response to a changing environment will enter once again into a stage of maturity. During this phase, the changes and innovations that were initiated during the renewal stage in the areas of service, governance, and administration will need to be integrated, stabilized, evaluated, and consolidated—always with one eye on the continually changing environment.

In fact, a successful and healthy organization will alternate between periods of renewal/revitalization and maturity/stabilization.

To visualize the lifecycles of a nonprofit organization, imagine a "Slinky" toy gently stretched out. Organizations move through a continuous cyclical pattern of innovation and consolidation (renewal and stabilization)—never coming back to the same place twice, but always moving forward.

When the "Slinky" Comes Uncoiled

There are two additional mini-stages in the lifecycle of a charitable organization. The healthiest of organizations will skim or skip through these phases without taking a lengthy or costly detour. These mini-phases are also known as "transition" points.

Transitions occur at the point where a mature organization—recognizing its need to adapt—begins the process of renewal. Conversely, another transition occurs as the organization begins to stabilize or consolidate the innovations it has adopted during the renewal stage.

By not responding quickly enough to changes in the environment—particularly the funding environment—organizations can slip into a kind of "free fall": funding plummets, the participation and enthusiasm of volunteers wanes, the leaders grow tired and frustrated, and management is operating in coast mode.

A charity slipping into "free fall" is not unlike a ship springing a leak—unless the leak is found and plugged quickly and effectively, the damage to the ship will increase. The longer an organization takes to recognize that it has bypassed a critical transition point without making appropriate adjustments, the longer it will take and the more resources it will consume to pull the organization back into a healthy lifecycle pattern.

Therefore, it is vitally important for the philanthropist to beware of investing heavily in an organization that has not recognized or responded to the fact that the world in which it operates has changed. Charitable investors are strongly urged to carefully examine an organization's written strategic plan before contributing heavily. Is the organization cognizant and prepared for what is up ahead, and have the managers developed a plan for successfully traveling through the anticipated changes?

Confronting Crisis

The other mini-stage, the phase one hopes no organization ever experiences, is that of "crisis." Crisis can occur at any time during an organization's lifecycle, and can take several forms:

- *Crisis of leadership* (for example, the untimely or unexpected death, resignation, or termination of one of the charity's key leaders)
- *Operational crisis* (for example, gross mismanagement of the organization's resources or a lawsuit against the nonprofit, draining it financially)
- *Crisis in the environment* (for example, a change in the economy that substantially impacts the organization's funding stream, such as a drop in the stock market in communities where substantial donor support comprised transfers of appreciated investments)

The philanthropist should be very careful about investing during a period of crisis. Chapter 6 will address how and when to consider providing emergency funding so that it will pose the lowest risk for your charitable investment.

Size as a Risk Factor

In assessing your comfort level with a charity's organizational culture, as well as in determining the level of philanthropic "risk" you are willing to accept, an important factor to consider is the size of the organization.

The smaller organization allows for the possibility of a relatively modest philanthropic investment to have a significant impact. Small charities can also provide the greatest opportunity for a high level of personal recognition and community appreciation. And finally, in the smaller organization, the leadership generally encourages—or at least does not discourage—active involvement by major donors in an advisory capacity.

In a mid-sized organization, the philanthropic donor can enjoy a higher degree of anonymity if he or she so chooses, and still achieve a relatively significant impact on the community through the support of this established organization. An organization of moderate size, however, will generally prefer not to involve the donor in key organizational or programmatic decisions unless the donor also serves on the board of directors.

Large organizations, by virtue of their size, show evidence of having a successful track record. For that reason, making a contribution to a large organization is very comfortable for many donors—they have a sense that their charitable investment is at very low risk. After all, in order to become a large organization, the charity needed to convince many donors and other supporters that the operation is sound, its efforts are worthwhile, and it is here to stay for the long term. This makes for a comfortable place where charitable investors can donate their funds.

Another low-risk charitable investment opportunity can be found in organizations having a dual national/local chapter structure. In some ways this may represent the soundest opportunity for a charitable investor.

On one hand, because contributions can be directed for use in the local community, donors are able to keep an eye on their investment and observe the tangible results of their gift. At the same time, the donors have a sense of assurance that the local chapter is operating to certain standards of sound management, leadership, and decision making because of the oversight provided by the national umbrella organization.

Do not accept this assumption at face value. This is not always the case. Donors would be well-advised to investigate the exact relationship between a local chapter and national umbrella organization when considering making a gift to such a charity.

When giving at the national level, donors may feel less connected to the organization to which they are contributing. But if chosen carefully, a national organization may bear the greatest fruit when it comes to effecting policy or system change. If that is the "sphere of influence" you have selected for your philanthropic investments, nationally or regionally based organizations will have the greatest impact.

Finally, there is the option of providing funding to an international organization. There are two basic alternatives for international giving. You can contribute to an organization that operates solely in a country other than the one in which you reside. Alternatively, you can invest in a domestically based organization that operates across borders and in many countries (for example, the International Red Cross).

Because the laws and traditions governing the charitable sector in other countries may vary widely from the standards that have been set in your home country, it is important to thoroughly understand how your contribution will be utilized and monitored by an international organization. This is why many contributions made to specific foreign nations are made primarily through faith-based institutions (e.g., churches or religious groups). Donors generally feel more secure when channeling their support through an organization with which they are already comfortable or familiar.

Organizational Budget as a Risk Indicator

Another means for assessing the level of philanthropic risk represented by your choice of charity is to look at the organization's budget. Because of financial scandals that were uncovered in several major national organizations in the United States a few years back, donors began to realize that there may be some distinct advantages to making their charitable investments in organizations of very modest means.

For example, if an organization is capable of performing a tremendous service in the community, affecting a large number of people, using innovative means and methods, and doing so with an annual operating budget under $100,000, it is highly unlikely that there is a lot of "slack" in the budget or a mismanagement of funds. A charitable investment of virtually any size in an organization with that profile can have quite a dramatic impact on the community, as well as on the organization's ability to build support from other funders.

That is not to say that organizations operating with significantly higher budgets—whether it is $2 million, $5 million, $20 million, or $100 million—are less effective or more wasteful. It may be true, however, that organization relatively "well off" compared with the rest of the nonprofit sector may be a little less cost-conscious in their approach to solving society's problems.

In fact, one of the key problems we see in the largest organizations in the charitable sector is the same problem that we see in many of our largest business corporations. Innovation and respect for human resources as an organization's most valuable assets are replaced by a misguided belief that the simple application of funds to a problem will solve that problem.

How Important—Really—Is Money?

❦

Treating money as the problem
is like blaming the thermometer for your fever.
—*Stephen Chapman*
❦

Ask most nonprofits operating today to name their single largest problem, and they will tell you that it is a lack of money. In the charitable sector, however, lack of money is rarely the real problem. The money problem is only a symptom.

Organizations with outstanding leadership, sound management, a strong mission, effective programs and services reflective of that mission, and a welcoming attitude toward new constituents (donors, volunteers, and clients alike) do not suffer money problems. It is when one of those key elements is out of sync that an organization begins to feel the pain financially.

That is why a large and wealthy organization can often operate at less than optimum performance levels before realizing that there are internal organizational problems. Financial "comfort" can act as a mask—even to the leaders of an organization—obscuring very real problems of governance, administration, or service until well past a point where the problem would be simple to address.

For that reason, the larger the gift and/or the wealthier the organization, the more critical it becomes for a philanthropic investor to have specific knowledge about the way in which that investment will be applied. As a donor, you want to ensure that your contribution will not serve as a temporary patch on a tire that's fundamentally shot, only to let the organization wobble down the road a little further.

Summary

Just as in financial investing, a philanthropic investor should come to terms with the level of investment risk with which he or she will feel comfortable—before committing to a major contribution. The "risk" factor in the charitable environment can be assessed by examining the organization's overall operational size, its budget, and its current stage of development.

In terms of organizational lifecycles, the charity that is in the emerging stage or in the renewal/revitalization stage represents the highest level of risk for the philanthropic investor. In many instances, however, those charities provide opportunity for the greatest social return on investment.

An organization in the maturing stage offers a sound, lower-risk investment for the philanthropist.

The charitable investor should take great care when considering a contribution to an organization that is either in transition or in crisis.

Note: See **Appendix B: Nonprofit Diagnostic Review** for determining the health and lifecycle stage of a nonprofit organization.

Chapter 6

How Will Your Money Be Used?

❦

When you write the checks,
you get the power to change things.
—*Jeffrey D. Jacobs*

❦

o place your charitable investment most effectively, your funds should be targeted for a specific kind of use by the organization you have selected as the beneficiary.

All Money Is Not the Same

There are essentially eight types of funding that a charity needs in order to fulfill its mission and deliver its programs and services while ensuring the long-term fiscal stability of its operation.

Capital Support

This is funding that an organization seeks in order to build a new facility, expand its current facility, or purchase major equipment, land, or buildings. An organization will typically seek the largest gifts first, eventually working its way down through progressively lower levels of giving, until it has achieved its overall capital campaign goal. Frequently, those donors making the largest gifts, known as "lead gifts," are offered an opportunity to have the building, or a section of the building, named in their honor.

Many donors find capital funding a highly gratifying form of philanthropy for two reasons. First, the donor can be confident that the support provided is being used in a tangible and necessary fashion, as evidenced by the actual construction of the facility or the purchase of equipment. Secondly, donors seeking long-term and highly visible recognition can ensure that their memory, or that of the person they choose to honor, will remain visible for a long, long time.

In the right setting, the building or facility may even become synonymous with the donor's name, as in the case of institutions such as the Norris Cancer Research Center, the Dorothy Chandler Pavilion, the Annenberg Center for Health Sciences, or the Getty Museum.

Endowment Funds

Endowment monies are funds that are invested in order to provide future, long-term support for the organization. Providing endowment funding is a charitable "investment" in the most real sense, for the return is both long-term and ongoing. In essence, endowment funds generate interest revenue on an annual basis, which the nonprofit may choose to utilize in a number of fashions. For example, a portion of the annual endowment revenue may be used to cover the charity's operating or overhead expenses. Or, those funds might be utilized to initiate or expand programs and services. The revenue can also be used for capital renovations, or extraordinary organizational needs. Most often smaller- and mid-sized organizations (those few in this size category that actually have an endowment) invest the generated proceeds back into the endowment, thereby growing its principal.

Endowment funding can be provided on an unrestricted basis. That is, the donor allows the charity to choose how it will utilize the endowment and the revenue generated by it. This decision is one most appropriately made by the board of directors or trustees.

Or, a donor may choose to restrict the use of the funding that he or she provides for an endowment to a specific purpose. For example, to "endow a chair" at a university is to provide funding that will generate revenue to meet or subsidize the salary requirements for that particular faculty position. Alternatively, one can endow a program or specific project in order to ensure that there will be an ongoing stream of revenue to maintain that program for the long term.

In some cases it is possible to request or negotiate the naming of a building, wing, or program in recognition for a substantial endowment gift, even if that endowment is not specifically related to the naming opportunity.

General Operating Support

Operating funds are those that are needed to cover the daily costs involved in running a charity and its programs. Operating monies cover those expenses that, although necessary, are not specifically or directly related to a program or service. For example, an organization that provides volunteer assistance to local schools may have only limited expenses directly related to that service. However, the organization maintains the central office from which staff solicit and assign volunteers. Their overhead costs may include rent, telephone expenses, postage, photocopying, electricity, heating and air conditioning, paper clips, rubber bands, basic furniture, and a computer. The chair, the desk, and the paper clips are not technically program-specific expenses, but the organization couldn't do business without them.

It is very difficult for organizations to raise general operating funds. Donors, both individual and foundations, are reluctant to provide funding that does not have an immediate and visible impact on the population they wish to benefit. As a result, many very fine nonprofit agencies may be adequately funded for their programs and services, but are struggling to survive because of the difficulty in securing funds to meet their overhead expenses.

A philanthropist considering making a gift of general operating funds can maximize that investment by guaranteeing operational support for a multi-year period. A one-year contribution may result in the organization facing the same lack of general operating support the following year and the donor realizing virtually no return on his or her investment. In tandem with providing longer-term operating support, the charitable investor should encourage, and perhaps require, that organizations receive technical assistance and training to help diversify their fundraising activities such that they will be able to maintain the necessary level of operational support in the years to come.

Seed Money/Pilot Money

This is money that an organization needs in order to undertake a new project or service, or in some cases to start up an entirely new nonprofit. Clearly a gift of seed or pilot money is a highrisk investment—there is no track record that the philanthropist can review in order to determine whether the organization is likely to be successful in its new endeavor.

On the other hand, the philanthropist has the opportunity to get in on the "ground floor" of what may be an extremely dynamic and highly effective initiative.

With seed or pilot money, it is absolutely critical—perhaps more so than with any other type of funding—to investigate the leadership, fiscal stability, program methodology, evaluation plans, and other sources of support before making an investment decision.

Program Funds

These are funds that are used in order to finance an ongoing program or service. Ideally, this funding will be used to expand program capabilities or reach, to increase the number of persons benefiting from an existing initiative, or to improve the overall quality of an existing service.

Providing ongoing program funds is a very low-risk proposition. Presumably there is a track record of success showing charitable investors that the application of their funds to the program will achieve the results the donors have specified. Further, ongoing programs generally have multiple sources of support, which means that other charitable investors have evaluated this organization and program and determined it to be worthy.

69

Although a safe investment, the donors may not see as significant an impact on the community as they might through the funding of a new initiative.

Recognition may be another factor to consider. Unless the level of financial support for a program is extraordinary, or is committed over a long period of time, recognition of the donors' gift may be somewhat modest.

Matching/Challenge Funds

This is funding that the philanthropist provides for use by the organization as its "magnet" money. In other words, the donor is not only providing a contribution to the organization to serve the organization's needs relative to operational costs, capital costs, or program costs, but is also giving the organization use of the money for the purpose of attracting other investors.

How does this work? As a donor who may be interested in supporting, for example, local literacy programs, it is not unlikely that three or four organizations might approach you with a request for funds. All things being equal—that is, the fiscal stability of the organization, the quality and commitment of its leadership, the successful track record of the program, and a solid base of support in the community—the wise investor will make his or her charitable contribution to that organization where that investment might be worth literally double its value.

Most organizations will be able to promise only that "if you give us one dollar, we will provide one dollar's worth of service to the community." However, the charity with a matching grant from another donor can make the statement that "if you give us one dollar, it will be matched by one dollar from another donor who has given us a special grant for this purpose. Therefore, with your one dollar contribution, we will be able to provide two dollars' worth of service to the community." By structuring your gift as a challenge or matching gift, you as a donor can double the value of your investment.

There is a slight difference between a matching fund and a challenge fund, although the two terms are often used interchangeably. In a matching situation, the donor agrees that for each dollar raised, up to specified limits, the donor will "match" that gift at some ratio. (For example, with a 1:1 ratio, for each dollar raised by the organization, the donor will provide one dollar.) Therefore, if the donor provides a matching grant in the amount of $10,000, with a 1:1 matching ratio, the donor will have to provide funding equal to the amount raised by the charity from other sources up to that $10,000 limit. In a matching grant situation, if the organization is able to raise only $9,999, the donor matches with $9,999.

With a challenge grant, the donor specifies a target amount that the organization must raise before the donor will provide corresponding funds on the basis of some ratio. For example, the donor may issue a challenge grant of $10,000, with a 1:1 ratio. When, and only when, the organization raises $10,000 from other sources will the donor provide his or her grant of $10,000. In a challenge situation, if the charity raises only $9,999, the donor can choose to give nothing, as the charity has not met the challenge.

Matching and challenge funding is very exciting for the philanthropic investor. First of all, it is a very low-risk investment. To enter into a matching or challenge arrangement, a charity must be confident that its programs and services are so strong that they will be attractive to other funders. The charity must also be confident that it is proficient enough in its fundraising methodologies that it will raise as much money as is necessary in order to meet the matching target or the challenge goal.

Just as the other donors whose funds will be solicited to meet your match will have doubled their investment value, so, too, will your contribution be doubled in value. Further, by requiring that an organization stretch its abilities and capabilities in the fund development arena, the philanthropist is strengthening the infrastructure of that charity such that its long-term health and success are ensured. Thus, the matching or challenge grant provides a variety of returns for the charitable investor.

Emergency Funds

Undoubtedly, this is a very risky form of charitable investment. There can be only two types of emergencies that an organization might face in its lifetime.

One is an emergency caused by a force outside of the control or influence of the charitable entity. For example, a hurricane, tornado, or earthquake destroys an organization's facility. Clearly, the charity had no way of foreseeing that this might happen, and probably is not in a financial position to address an emergency of that magnitude out of its general funds.

In such case, a charitable gift of emergency funding can have a double effect. First, there is the immediate impact that the emergency funds will have on the lives of the people served by the endangered organization: the hungry, the homeless, the battered, students, the ill, etc. Moreover, when natural disaster strikes, programs and services already operating at full capacity tend to become strained by the additional number of community members who have also been affected by these catastrophic circumstances.

Without emergency funding, disaster can also spell the end for an effective and much-needed charity. Shutting down due to catastrophe is like watching the railroad tracks simply end.

A gift of emergency funding not only impacts the lives of individuals in the community at that moment, but it can ensure the ongoing existence of a charitable organization so that it can continue to serve for years and generations to come.

Beware, however, the other category of "emergency." This is the emergency that is wholly human and generally manifests itself as an announcement that the doors will close next week (or next month) because the charity has run out of cash. This type of emergency is no emergency at all. It is simply proof that someone at the charity "fell asleep at the switch." And that "someone," almost without fail, is the board of the organization. No charity comes that near to its doors closing without red flags appearing at least six to eight months in advance of the emergency. Those signs would have been evident in the organization's financial statements, staff morale, word of mouth in the community, and a host of other means that would be difficult to ignore.

To invest emergency funds in an organization suffering from a human emergency is to risk throwing good money after bad. Only in very rare circumstances should a philanthropist consider making a substantial gift to an organization that has clearly mismanaged its resources prior to this point.

These circumstances would include situations in which the failure or shutdown of the organization would severely impair the well-being or quality of life for a major segment of the community's population. Further, the longer the charity has been in existence, the more likely it is that the organization will be able to muster the internal resources—as well as the broad base of community support—that it will need if it is to be helped over this hump.

Lastly and most importantly, it is absolutely critical that before any emergency funding is committed, the board of directors or some subset of that group must detail an actionable strategic plan that is designed not only to pull the charity from the brink of disaster, but to ensure the establishment of a solid foundation for ongoing long-term success.

From experience, we can tell you that in a human emergency rarely will one find the unique set of circumstances that would warrant a philanthropic infusion of funding. Just as a giraffe is not able to change its spots, so, too, is it difficult for a group of trustees to change the patterns, thinking, and decision-making habits that led to imminent disaster.

Loans/Investments

In this complex form of charitable giving, the philanthropist may choose to support an organization or project in which traditional financial institutions would be unwilling to invest, or for which they would charge interest rates prohibitive for a charity. Although this type of funding is not initially structured as an outright gift, the donor may choose to convert it to such at any point he or she desires.

For example, a highly successful, fast-growing, and much-needed charity may be in desperate need to expand its facility as quickly as possible. Delaying construction until the funding can be raised through a traditional capital campaign may create an unacceptable burden on the client population. In such a situation, a charity may seek to borrow funding so that construction can commence even while contributions are being sought. Commercial lenders, if even interested in lending money to a charity, will most likely have to charge competitive market rates, which would be prohibitive for most nonprofit organizations.

In such an instance, the philanthropist could offer to provide the much-needed support to the charity in the form of a low-interest loan. Clearly, the donor would want to perform due diligence on the organization, its leaders, and its financial history. If all is in order, the charitable investor can have a major impact on the community through his or her gift of support, as well as get back that funding to use for assisting that same or another organization.

Clearly, there is some risk involved here. The organization, feeling "secure" because of the loan, may not be as aggressive as it otherwise would be in pursuing contributed funds. Further, should the fortunes of the organization change over time such that it is unable to meet debt service, the philanthropist will be in the awkward position of deciding how and at what level of intensity to pursue remuneration.

Therefore, it is critical that the charitable investor and the leaders of the nonprofit organization are clear and candid with one another with respect to terms, conditions, expected communications, and consequences relative to repayment ... and that they put it in writing!

Summary

Direct financial support to a charitable organization can take a variety of different forms. Some of these offer a lower or higher risk factor, as well as varying rates of "philanthropic return." Some forms of support are more appropriate in the context of a short-term relationship with the organization. Other forms are sensible charitable investments only when conceived of as a long-term, ongoing relationship with the selected agency.

In either case, you must make your decision true to your own long-term vision for a better world, stronger community, or heightened quality of life for other people.

Part Three

Investigating Opportunities for Your Charitable Investment

Chapter 7

Finding a Charity That Shares Your Goals

❦

Human beings, who are almost unique
in having the ability to learn from the experience of others,
are also remarkable
for their apparent disinclination to do so.

—Douglas Adams

❦

How do you begin to look for a charitable organization that shares your vision and your goals? The first step is to review the decisions you've already made following the guidelines set out in the previous chapters:

- Drawing on your personal history, in which field of service would you like to focus your philanthropy?
- What is the sphere of influence or desired level of impact you wish to have through your charitable giving: personal, community, institutional, or policy?
- Which is the community you have chosen to benefit through your contributions?

- Have you defined the level of "investment risk" with which you will feel most comfortable?
- Have you determined whether you would like your contribution to constitute a substantial portion of a smaller budget or operation? Or would you feel as comfortable starting with a small or moderate contribution to an organization of a size where your contribution might receive less recognition?

Once you have answered these questions as specifically as possible to your own and your family's satisfaction, only then can you start to identify and investigate organizations whose work and profiles most closely match your philanthropic investment objectives.

Where to Start

The best way to start is by speaking to other "investors." By this, we mean you should contact other individuals, organizations, or institutions that provide substantial funding to a broad range of nonprofits—or advise nonprofits—at least some of which may fall in the category that you would like to support.

Community Foundations

Community foundations are a great resource and can be found across the country. In essence, community foundations are organized to benefit charities and people who live within a specified geographic area. For example, the California Community Foundation is organized to benefit nonprofits and communities throughout the state of California. The Community Foundation of Riverside County, on the other hand, is organized to benefit agencies only within that specific county. Many cities have their own community foundations.

Community foundations are charities set up specifically to manage and distribute charitable funds that are generally also drawn from the geographic region that they benefit. Consequently, community foundations function as an objective resource for information on a broad range of agencies and organizations within the region that they serve.

Community foundations receive numerous proposals for support from organizations within their community. Part of the foundations' function is to evaluate not only those proposals, but the organizations that have submitted them. As a result, community foundations have their finger on the pulse of the nonprofit sector within that specified region, and can be a wonderful source for information on who is doing what, who is doing it well, and who is in need and deserving of support.

Further, the community foundation may have specific information about a given organization in that community that may help you to determine whether or not to consider a contribution to or investment in that particular charity.

A community foundation may also be able to let you know whether there is an existing nonprofit, project, or initiative that matches the profile of the work you would like to support.

Or, perhaps you have identified an unmet need in your chosen community. The community foundation can be a wonderful resource to help you determine whether and how to launch your *own* charitable initiative.

Grant-Making Organizations

Another source of information on charitable groups that meet your investment goals are other grant-making organizations. Most frequently, these organizations are private, independent foundations sponsored by individuals or families who are seriously involved in charitable giving.

The most prominent alliance of such foundations is the Council of Foundations. The Council is a membership organization of foundations across the country that are organized into smaller, regional entities known as Regional Associations of Grantmakers (RAGs). For example, one prominent RAG is the Southern California Association for Philanthropy.

Contact a local regional association of grantmakers and let them know about your particular charitable giving interests. They can direct you to member foundations that fund similar activities.

You can contact these and other foundations that fund or support activities or projects of the type in which you are interested, and thus start developing your own list of prospects.

Technical Assistance Centers

Another excellent resource for information on organizations and initiatives are the many technical assistance centers located throughout the country. These are generally nonprofit organizations whose mission is to provide education, consultation, training, and other resources to nonprofit organizations. Nonprofit technical assistance organizations interface with large numbers of charities on a regular, often daily basis. They operate very closely with the nonprofit community and therefore are often the most knowledgeable source about a local community's nonprofit sector, about changing or unmet needs within a particular community, and about the effectiveness of specific organizations.

Technical assistance agencies can take many forms. In some communities the Volunteer Center is the major resource for nonprofits. In other communities it may be known as the Support Center. The network of technical assistance providers includes a wide range of organizations, many of which belong to or are members of the Nonprofit Management Association.

The local United Way chapter in the community that you would like to benefit may be a source of information about organizations doing work of the type you are interested in funding. At the very least, the United Way should be able to direct you to the nearest community foundation, Regional Association of Grantmakers, or technical assistance provider.

Experts

Another wonderful source of leads are "experts in the field." These may be academic professionals, consultants, or practitioners in the field who are highly knowledgeable about those organizations and institutions that are engaged in cutting-edge, exemplary, or highly effective work. Check with universities located in the area you wish to benefit to see whether they have a degree or certificate program in philanthropy or nonprofit management. Contact their faculty and lecturers for recommendations on charities matching your interest profile.

How to Use These Resources

More important than what you *ask* them will be what you *tell* them. First, be sure that you are talking to the right person. Generally the "right person" will be the executive director and, once the receptionist understands that you are a potential donor looking for assistance, there should be no problem in having your call put through to the appropriate party.

Let your contact know specifically what kinds of initiatives you would like to support through your charitable contributions. Include all the information that was reviewed earlier: the field of service, sphere of influence, community, and organization size and budget. The more specific you can be about your parameters, the more helpful they can be with suggestions or recommendations.

Ask if they know of any organizations whose work matches the profile you have described. Be sure that in their recommendation they include organizations that they have not been able to fund as well as organizations that they themselves have supported.

It is not unusual for a foundation to receive many more applications for funding than it can possibly accommodate. As a result, many fine nonprofits end up on the "declined" pile simply because the funder ran out of grant money.

In other cases, the foundation has set its guidelines very specifically, and numerous nonprofits doing very fine have their requests for funding rejected because their activities fall outside of the granting institution's current field of interest.

Do not look to these contacts for specific references, recommendations, or opinions on whether or not you should support any given organization. Rather, look to these sources to help you in compiling a list of charities to investigate yourself or to have investigated on your behalf.

Again, the key to putting together a strong list of candidates for your charitable investment is knowing precisely what it is you would like to accomplish with your philanthropic giving.

When There Is No Match

There are two routes you can follow should you find that there really are no charities doing the kind of work you would like to fund.

The simplest solution is to simply look harder. You may find that the kind of organization doing the work you wish to support falls into a "crack" such that it will not appear on the radar screen of the community foundation, a private foundation, a technical assistance center, or organizations such as the United Way.

In that case, one of the most effective ways to find those organizations is to "advertise." This is not to suggest that you should advertise in a general publication. However, there are a number of trade and professional journals and publications—both in print and now on-line—that serve the non-profit sector. Nonprofits serious about their work regularly read or review these major informational resources. These would include *The Chronicle of Philanthropy*, *Non Profit Times*, and *Contributions*, as well as a variety of other publications that can be found in Appendix C. Additionally, technical assistance providers, volunteer centers, and other such associations or alliances of nonprofits have their own newsletters or member communication devices.

All of these will be happy to post your listing of funds that you may have available for a particular type of project or organization.

In your ad, be as specific as possible in defining the type of project and organization from which you would like to hear. Be sure to request that responses be directed to a post office box provided by the publication, to the consultant you may have assisting you, or to some other "blind" mail box. This will ensure your privacy as well as screen you from the flood of responses such a notice can generate for some time to come.

Writing the Ad

In your notice, define the parameters within which a prospective beneficiary organization must fall: program type, location, size, exact population served, etc. Request an initial letter of inquiry— no longer than two pages—in which the organization is to describe its project or activity and how, exactly, it matches the profile that you have described in your advertisement.

Two pages provide ample space to provide critical information that would allow you to determine whether or not you wish to further investigate a charity. It also forces the organization to get right to the point about what it does, why it's valuable, and how it meets the criteria that you have stipulated.

Should any of the responding charities catch your interest, you should request further and more specific information from them. At this point, you would send them a more comprehensive description of your funding guidelines, as well as an in-depth application for them to complete. Samples of both can be found in Appendix F.

Avoid accepting "free form" narrative proposals. First, they can be murderously boring to wade through—without ever getting to the information that is of most importance to you. Also, it is easier to hide negative information in a barrage of other positive "stuff."

Going Off the Beaten Track

❧

Two roads diverged in a wood, and I—
I took the one less traveled by,
And that has made all the difference.
—Robert Frost

❧

It would seem that these methods and resources for finding non-profit organizations are the most effective in larger communities or metropolitan areas, or when trying to uncover fairly sophisticated or "known" organizations. Where do you begin the search when you are for looking for an organization that is, quite literally, "off the beaten track "?

If the kind of charity you are looking for is off the beaten track, it will be known to, at the very least, the individuals who serve as the board directors and volunteers for that charity. In smaller or rural communities, these persons often hold leadership positions in other community-based entities. Members of the local Chamber of Commerce, Rotary, Soroptimists, Lions, Elks, faith congregations, and other associations of highly involved community members can be great resources for finding organizations that may have a very low profile.

One can also research the names of all of the tax-exempt charitable organizations within a given state or ZIP code on the Internal Revenue Service's Web site. It lists any tax-exempt nonprofit that is required to file an annual informational tax return (Form 990). The IRS listings, however, provide only minimal information, which may or may not be of use in making your charitable investment decision.

Summary

Once you have defined the parameters for your charitable investments, it should not be difficult to find the names of and information about the organizations that match your investment profile.

The charitable community—and each of its sectors—is made up of generous individuals who will be happy to help you in your quest to find those organizations doing the type and quality of work that you are anxious to support.

Note: The following appendices provide information regarding the issues raised in this chapter:

- **Appendix C: Associations, Publications, and Web Sites Serving Philanthropists**
- **Appendix D: Comprehensive Directory of Grantmaking Associations**
- **Appendix E: Community Foundations**
- **Appendix F: Sample Foundation Guidelines Information Sheet**
- **Appendix G: Sample Funding Application**

Chapter 8

Look Before You Leap: Performing Due Diligence

❦

*"I've know everyone on the Board for years,
and they're great people."*
"The organization seems to do good work."
*"I've always seen them in the paper.
They must be a worthy cause."*
*"Well, it's a national charity
that's been around forever.... By giving to them,
I know where my money goes!"*

❦

ut, what do you *really* know?

■ How many of us knew a few years back that the chief executive of the most prosperous and respected federated campaign organization in the nation was using substantial agency funds to further his relationships with various women—among other improper and illegal uses of our contributions?

- Were the residents of one small community aware that nearly a quarter of their senior service agency's annual budget had been embezzled?
- Would you have invested several hundred thousand dollars of your funds in short-term CDs? You probably didn't know that the officials of one well-respected regional charity chose this strategy for growing their reserve because they just didn't know any better.
- And if you knew, would you care that numerous high-visibility galas across this country net less money for programs and service than the combined price of the flowers, decorations, and entertainment for those galas?

As a donor, in most cases, you know only what a nonprofit wants you to know. And for good reason—nonprofits want and need your money. Yet philanthropists are not nearly as diligent about investigating charities as they are about analyzing comparably sized personal investment opportunities.

What do we mean when we urge you to perform due diligence on a nonprofit?

There are four main areas that are critical to determining whether or not a nonprofit organization represents a sound "risk" for your charitable contribution.

A. Mission and Programs

The charity's leaders should be absolutely clear about the essential nature of the organization's work, and how each and every program and service of the nonprofit is directly related to that mission.

The healthy organization will be concise and specific in addressing the following *mission*-related questions:

1. Who are we? Who constitutes the organization?
2. Whom do we seek to serve?
3. In what geographical area or communities do we provide our programs and services?
4. What vital, critical, urgent human need do we seek to address?

5. How do we serve this need differently than any other organization seeking to address this same issue?
6. In essence, what change in the world do we seek to make?
7. Why are we deserving of a donor's money?

Those charities that have a strong focus, a serious sense of purpose, and an overview of the "the big picture" will have no problem giving you a succinct answer to each of these questions. That's because the answers to these questions inform their daily work.

If an organization finds it simpler to "laundry list" their programs and services than to communicate an overarching mission, you may wish to take pause before making a substantial contribution there.

B. Programs and Services

It is important to determine whether an organization's programs and services are truly reflective of the values and priorities addressed in the overall mission of the organization. Programs and service do not equal mission. Rather, programs and services should be an expression of the overall mission in action. In gauging the strength of a charity's actual work, a prospective donor should ask these key *program*-related questions.

1. Does the organization seem to jump onto whatever "bandwagon" of service is popular with the public (or attractive to funders) at any given time, without really connecting it to the organization's mission or existing programs? This would indicate that resources are being applied to activities primarily on the basis of what's "fashionable" rather than what's effective or needed.
2. Does each program and service address a specific issue or need?
3. Does it address that need in a way that is effective and measurable?
4. Does the organization maintain an ongoing process of evaluation to assess whether its programs and services are in fact achieving the desired results?
5. Do the programs and services consume a disproportionately

small percentage of the nonprofit's resources relative to the expenditures being made for overhead, fund-raising events, and other "special" activities? In the strongest and most successful organizations, service will always be the priority.

In general, weak organizations are those with a very broad or unfocused mission, where programs seem to relate neither to the mission nor to the organization's other activities.

C. Quality and Commitment of the Leadership

This factor, more than any other, is underutilized as a major indicator of whether an organization is capable of and committed to achieving the objectives intended through your contribution.

By "leadership" we are referring to those individuals who hold the ultimate authority, the greatest responsibility, and the fiduciary obligation for a non-profit corporation: that leadership is the board of directors or board of trustees.

The executive director and the senior administrative staff members are all critical players. However, they are paid employees who function under the guidance and direction of the board. The board has—or should have—the ultimate power and control over the organization.

The *quality* of the board can and should be measured in several different ways:

1. Is the board of directors large enough to encompass the many types of expertise and representation that would be necessary for guiding an organization with this mission and this size budget? At the same time, is the board small enough that each director feels a compelling personal responsibility for the sound and ethical governance of the institution?
2. Does the board, in fact, have among its members professionals or experts knowledgeable in key areas such as finance, law, fund raising, and business management, as well as professionals and experts from the field(s) of the organization's primary

endeavor? For example, does the board of an educational institution have any educators on the board? Does an arts-oriented
charity have a practicing artist on the board? Are individual
board members actively engaged in committee work related to
the functional or operational areas in which they have expertise?

3. Does the board have members to act as both representatives
   and "ambassadors" to the many sectors of the community
   which the organization seeks to either serve or solicit? Do
   board members hold positions of visibility or authority else-
   where in the community such that their personal or professional stature enhances the image and reputation of the nonprofit?
4. Do board members take an active role in establishing policy,
   the strategic plan, and a long-term vision for the organization?

Evaluating the *commitment* of the leadership is another matter:

1. Do all members of the board of directors or trustees meet on
   a regular and consistent basis appropriate to the scope, level,
   and nature of work required to successfully direct an organization of its size?
2. When meeting as a board, do these "stewards" of the organization focus their attention and discussions on those matters
   requiring policy-level attention? Or do they spend their time
   together discussing matters more appropriate to the staff?
3. Does each board member have a clear understanding of the
   specific reason they were asked to serve on the board and
   what their unique role on the board is at this time? Is that
   understanding reflected in each board member's assignment
   to and participation in committee work?
4. Has each board member made an annual financial contribution to the organization at a level reflective of the priority that
   organization's work holds in that director's life?

This issue of determining whether every board member contributes financially to the organization should be critical to your
own donation decision.

Would you make a major investment in a company or venture
in which the owners and founders had no stake? You would at

least think twice before putting money into the firm, and you would probably maintain some level of oversight or control over that investment once it was made.

Yet every day, philanthropists and major donors make significant contributions to charities without verifying the participation of the "owners" (i.e., board members).

There is a good reason why many institutional funders—foundations and corporations—demand to know what percentage of directors on a given board contribute to that charity.

They know that board members managing their own contributions as well as those of the public will often be more deliberate in their financial and planning decisions. The internal standards of accountability are often higher when board members' own money is at stake.

What should be more telling to the discriminating donor, however, is the fact of whether board members give at all.

In a recent survey of one hundred nonprofits with annual budgets ranging from $100,000 to $4 million and with boards sized 3 to 30, *less than 10%* reported that each member of the board had made a monetary gift beyond the purchase of an event ticket or some other exchange-for-value contribution.

The size of contribution is almost irrelevant—for some trustees, a donation of $10 might constitute a personal sacrifice, where for others a gift of $10,000 would be simple. A financial contribution is a tangible sign of a director's faith in the organization, its mission, its leadership, and its direction.

Before making your charitable investment, inquire about the board's donation track record. Then decide if you would trust them to manage *your* money.

D. Financial Stability

Just as with any investment opportunity, when considering a substantial charitable contribution, it is critical that the philanthropist examine key financial indicators for the organization:

1. Does the organization engage an independent, certified public accounting firm or professional on an annual basis to prepare audited financial statements? If not, does the organization have a compilation prepared by an accounting professional on an annual basis?
2. Does the organization consistently establish and approve an annual operating budget *prior* to the beginning of each fiscal year? Is that budget tracked in relation to actual expenditures and income over the course of the year? Is a variance report prepared and distributed to each board member on a regular basis? Does each board member understand how to read and interpret the organization's financial documents? Are the financial documents used as decision-making tools? Or are they organizational "window dressing"?
3. Has the organization run in the black consistently for the last three years? If there has been a substantial surplus, how has the board of directors chosen to utilize those funds? If the organization is running a deficit, is this a first-time deficit? Or has the organization been operating at a loss for an extended period of time? If this is a first-time deficit, is there a clear understanding or explanation on the part of the board for why and how this occurred? Has the board developed a written plan to ensure that the deficit situation does not repeat itself in the coming fiscal year?
4. Does the organization maintain any type or types of reserve funds, such as a capital reserve or an endowment fund? If so, who is responsible for overseeing or investing those funds in order to maximize their value? Does the organization have a written and regularly updated investment policy?

E. Other Individuals or Entities That Have "Invested" in This Organization

If the organization has been successful in attracting financial support from other individuals whose judgment you respect, or from institutional funders such as foundations or corporations that have rigorous standards and requirements in order to qualify for funding, the "risk" to your investment diminishes. This is true also if the organization has successfully negotiated a loan process with a commercial lender.

The key questions relative to other investors include:

1. What other major donors or funders have undertaken a comprehensive assessment of this organization and have deemed it worthy of a substantial financial contribution?
2. Whom can you contact to verify those funders' or donors' findings?

If you have been approached or are considering becoming an early contributor to a new organization or campaign, there may be very little "investor" history for you to reference. In that case, you must take special care in assessing the other three factors: mission, leadership, and overall fiscal stability.

Now that you know *what* to evaluate in a due diligence process, how do you actually go about *performing* due diligence? And how can you go about investigating a nonprofit that may be located geographically at some distance from you?

Performing Due Diligence

You have one objective in performing due diligence: to ensure that the organization in which you are considering making a charitable investment is capable of and committed to using your investment as effectively as possible to accomplish your personal philanthropic objectives.

Again, the major factors you will be assessing are the agency's mission and programs, its financial stability, the quality and commitment of the organization's leadership, and the confidence level of its other "investors."

There are three methods for performing the due diligence. One method relies solely on an examination of key organizational documents. The other two methods combine comprehensive in-person and on-site examinations with document analysis.

Method One: Document Analysis

Step 1. Initial Telephone Contact

Contact the executive director of the organization about which you would like more information. Say that his or hers is one of a number of organizations under consideration for a substantial charitable contribution. Ask the director to send you a letter no more than two pages in length providing essential information about the organization: what it does, who it serves, what social issue or problem it addresses, and how it does so in a fashion unique from other agencies.

Make note of the way in which you were handled on the telephone. Were all members of the staff with whom you spoke courteous, pleasant, and responsive? Was there a major change in how you were dealt with once your interest as a potential donor became known? If you were someone needing services from this agency, would you feel equally welcomed and comfortable in calling?

Step 2. Review of Letter Responses

Set aside any letters whose content indicates that the organization or its work do not match the focus you have selected for your philanthropic giving. You should send a brief courtesy note to such agencies, thanking them for their response and letting them know that, at this point in time, you are unable to make a contribution. We often suggest sending a modest donation to those organizations as a means of showing your general support for their work, while making it clear that a larger contribution is not forthcoming at this time. (Surprisingly, some organizations have been so compelling in their appreciation for even this modest contribution that philanthropists re-consider their decision and do end up pursuing a longer-term and more generous relationship!)

For those organizations that have impressed you with their response and responsiveness to your inquiry—and whose profiles seems to match your personal philanthropic interest as determined earlier—it is time to submit a complete proposal.

Step 3. Request for Proposal

Prepare a standard form letter to send to those organizations which seem a strong match for your funding interests, requesting that they submit a proposal consisting of the following items *only*:

- A *brief overview* of the organization's *history* and *mission.*
- A *brief overview* of the *specific program, service, or project* that you as the prospective donor are interested in possibly supporting. This should include information on that initiative's "track record" (if it is an ongoing activity), the number of people served by that program, and a clear explanation of the organization's method of evaluating the success of that particular activity.
- In the case of an ongoing program, a copy of the *actual expense and revenue report* for that *specific program* for the last completed fiscal year, as well as the *projected program budget* for the current or coming fiscal year. In the case of a new program or service, the agency should send you the *projected budget* for that activity for the coming fiscal year.
- If you are considering a gift toward general operating support, a capital campaign contribution, or a donation to an endowment fund, request *current financial statements* relevant to that particular *fund or campaign.*
- A list of the *organization's board members*, as well as a brief paragraph about each, stating their professional affiliation (for example, "Vice President of Marketing for the ABC Corporation, a widget manufacturing firm") and, most important, the particular experience or expertise that each brings to this board. Ask that they note on which committee each individual serves. Finally, they should include the total (aggregate) amount of contributions made by that individual to the organization.
- A copy of the *complete audited financial statements* for the last fiscal year, as well as a copy of the *operating budget* for the current fiscal year. You will use these documents to verify whether there was a surplus or deficit last year and to determine whether "overhead" and fundraising expenditures were appropriate and in line with the requirements of the agency's programs and services. By comparing the last year's "actuals" with this year's projection, you should be able to tell whether their numbers are heading up, down, or remaining stable—and whether the board is realistic in its financial planning.

- Copies of *minutes* from the *last three board meetings*. Any sensitive information may be blocked out. These key corporate documents will give you a strong idea of what is currently happening internally and what matters the leaders of the organization are choosing to focus on.
- A list of *major contributors*—individual, corporate, and foundation—for the *last eighteen months,* including *sizes of contribution* and *contact information*.
- A copy of the organization's *determination letter of tax-exempt status*—501[c](3)—from the Internal Revenue Service, which will ensure that your contribution would be tax-deductible as a charitable contribution.

Lest you be inundated with "stuff" produced by the organization for purely promotional reasons, request that the nonprofit not send any additional materials, such as brochures, videotapes, press releases, or testimonials.

Once you have received the complete proposal package containing only those materials requested, review each document carefully, utilizing the due diligence standards outlined in the first half of this chapter with respect to mission, fiscal stability, leadership, and other "investors."

To Tell the Truth ...

Grant- and proposal-writing has become somewhat of a "game" for many nonprofits. They know that if they present themselves well on paper, they increase their chances of "winning" your financial support. Therefore, the motivation is high to present a highly favorable—and sometimes misleading—picture of the agency's overall effectiveness and stability. Many nonprofits will "shade" their case and their statistics to secure the funding they need to remain in operation.

Will you catch them all by examining the documentation requested? Probably not. But you will substantially decrease the likelihood of making your contribution to an organization that will waste it.

That is why, if at all possible, you should consider combining an in-person, on-site investigation with document analysis when considering any type of substantial gift.

Method Two: Visiting the Organization

Step 1. Arranging for the On-Site Visit

You can gather an enormous amount of information from a visit to the organization to which you are considering a contribution. You can see the operation in action. You can get a feel for the level of experience and expertise among the staff. Staff and volunteer morale can be observed. And most importantly, client/agency interaction can be assessed.

Should an on-site visit be announced or unannounced? The increasing incidence of site visits by prospective funders has led to the development of well-choreographed "performances" by agencies anxious to secure funding. In some respects, site visits are becoming a less reliable means for verifying an organization's strengths.

Ideally, after receiving and reviewing the proposal package, you would notify the organization's executive director that you would like to visit sometime during a specified one- or two-week period. Verify the agency's hours of operation and the general availability of the executive director during that period. Unless you have no alternative, try to avoid setting a specific time or date on which you will visit. Your objective is to see the organization on a typical day, as opposed to a day on which everyone has been "warned" to be on best behavior.

Let the executive director know that, without being intrusive, you would like the opportunity to visit and chat with several people involved with the agency. Again, in the ideal situation, the executive director would give you the freedom to speak with individual staff members, volunteers, or clients outside of that executive's presence.

Step 2. Making the Site Visit

The site visit may require a trip to the administrative or organizational headquarters, as well as to the site where programs and services actually take place, if the two locations are not one and the same. For example, a Los Angeles-based team mentoring program has its administrative offices downtown, while the actual mentoring activities take place at various school sites located in the inner city. In a situation such as this, a visit to both locations would be valuable.

In general, on a site visit you are looking for evidence that the organization is running smoothly and in a highly organized fashion, and that its environment is one that is positive and constructive, and that encourages collaboration among administrators, volunteers, and staff.

You particularly want to observe whether any program or activity that you are considering funding is running according to the information that was shared with you in writing.

And most importantly, you will want to determine whether the individuals being served believe that the organization has their best interests at heart—is their interaction with the organization having an impact consistent with your philanthropic objectives?

Something as simple as the cleanliness of the facility can tell you whether or not this is an organization that you'd feel comfortable investing in. Has the environment been designed for the primary comfort of the staff or for the primary comfort of the people they are seeking to serve?

By speaking with volunteers and staff about the work they perform, you should get a feel for whether they are comfortable with the direction and management of the organization. In speaking with administrators, listen for indications that the staff, administration, and board of directors work in harmony with one another, that there is a clearly understood direction in which the organization is moving, and that there is a mutual respect for the professionalism of all parties.

Method Three: Meeting the Leaders in Person

Step 1. Arranging to Attend a Board Meeting

This is an enormously effective way to determine whether a specific nonprofit is one in which you would feel comfortable investing your charitable funds.

Again, in the ideal situation, your objective is to see the organization—in this case, its leaders—in action as they normally are, and not on best behavior. Therefore, let the executive director and the board president know that you would like to attend one of the board's next three meetings, and double-check those dates. Let them know that you understand the confidential nature of board discussions, and that you will honor that confidentiality when you attend. Also, let the executive director and board president know that, should any particularly sensitive matter arise that would not be appropriate for discussion before an outsider, you will, of course, excuse yourself.

Step 2. Attending the Board Meeting

As discussed earlier, the quality and commitment of the leaders of an organization is one of the most important factors influencing the long-term health and success of the charity.

The basics to observe when attending a board meeting would include whether all of the board members, or at least a vital majority, are in attendance. Do trustees show respect for the importance of the board's work by arriving promptly and starting on time?

Does the agenda for the meeting reflect the board's primary role as the organization's policy-setting body? Does the agenda comprise a series of issues requiring action and/or pertinent discussion? Or do board members simply read reports to the group? Do board members appear prepared? Warning: an agenda that consists exclusively of reports that are essentially read from materials that were previously mailed to trustees is usually a sign that the board is unsure of its role, is not clear about the responsibilities of governance, and is spending a minimum amount of attention on the agency outside of these meetings.

Does the meeting proceed in a timely and constructive fashion? Are all board members actively engaged in the discussion? Not all directors will necessarily speak on every issue, but at the very least each director should be closely following the ongoing discussion. Are there any board "bullies" who tend to dominate the meeting and the decision-making process? Are votes approached with serious consideration? Or do they often result in a half-hearted unanimity?

Is there evidence that committees are actively working? Are

they meeting on a regular basis? Are committee recommendations met with confidence on the part of the board? Or are committees second-guessed on their work?

Review the minutes from the last meeting. How was attendance at that meeting? Do the minutes reflect some continuity between the matters discussed and determined at the last meeting and the issues before the board at this meeting?

Are financial reports reviewed at the board meeting? Does it appear that all of the board members understand the financial documents? Is financial information referred to during the course of board discussions on other matters? Most important, does the financial information distributed at the board meeting correspond to the financial information that was provided to you as a prospective donor?

Be wary of investing in an organization where the board seems relatively uninformed or dispassionate about the organization's programs and services. At the board meeting, observe carefully whether the board faithfully exercises its stewardship role or whether it abdicates that role to the executive director.

Does the board meeting seem unnecessarily long for the nature and seriousness of agenda items? Does the discussion stay on-point and focused on the agenda item? Do board discussions easily go off on tangential or insignificant matters? Beware of the board that spends an inordinate amount of time discussing the particulars of a special event or fund-raiser.

Does the board president exhibit strong leadership qualities, including a great respect for all of his or her board colleagues? Does the president manage the meeting in a fashion that ensures that everyone will be heard on all of the most critical topics?

Is it clear that there are other members of the board with strong leadership qualities such that there will be no vacuum in leadership in the immediate years to come?

A 90-minute investment of your time to attend a board meeting can be invaluable in assessing whether an organization and its leadership represent a sound investment of your charitable dollars.

If attending a board meeting is not feasible or is inconvenient, there is an alternative method for assessing the organization's leadership. This method can be used alone or in follow-up to your attendance at a board meeting

Alternative Method Three: Representative Board Group Interview

Most executive directors will be extremely well-versed about the ongoing operations and future plans of the organization. They will be intimately aware of the organization's financial situation, including its challenges and opportunities, as well as its prospects and plans for raising money. After all, that's their job.

Too often, board members are somewhat less aware of critical information with respect to the organization's mission, programs, finances, and future plans. It's not difficult to roust one or two "ringers" from the board who can impress a potential donor with their commitment to stewardship or knowledge of the organization. Finding the third is often what separates an organization with a strong board from an organization with a "letterhead" board.

Ask to meet with a group of, at minimum, three board members for the purpose of gaining a fuller understanding of the organization's direction and needs. A face-to-face meeting is most effective, but this meeting can also be arranged as a teleconference. Make it clear that the executive director is *not* to participate in this informal meeting. Naturally, your promise of confidentiality should be extended.

During the meeting, listen carefully for the board members' confidence and comfort levels in speaking knowledgeably when asked direct questions about:

1. The basic mission of the organization
2. The range of its programs and services
3. The organization's current financial state, as well as financial projections for the near and long term
4. The general salary range and benefits package of the executive director and key staff
5. The board's three most important objectives for the current fiscal year

6. The three greatest challenges facing the organization at this time

Remember, if you are going to enter into a partnership with this board of directors as a major donor seeking to achieve a specific philanthropic objective, it is critical that you and your potential partners can speak candidly to one another. In a fairly closed setting, with only a small group of board members present, are the trustees willing to share the good, the bad, and the "ugly" with you? Do you sense that there is an honesty and candor between you and these leaders? Or are they strictly trying to "sell" you on the organization in order to get your money?

Summary

Ultimately, all of these due diligence activities are designed to lead you to the answers to these three questions:

1. Are the leaders of this organization focused on a vision that is strongly aligned with the philanthropic objective you have set for yourself, your family, or your foundation?
2. Are the people at all levels within the organization—governing board, executive director and administrators, volunteers, and staff—in sync with one another and with this vision?
3. Do these people have the proven know-how and commitment to achieve that vision or objective through effective use of your proposed contribution?

Is it absolutely necessary for you to engage in all three methods of due diligence—document analysis, on-site visit, and meeting the leadership? Depending on the size of your proposed contribution, you may feel that a thorough review of the paperwork is satisfactory.

As with any investment opportunity or decision, however, the greater the sums involved, the more intensive the due diligence should be. You should see, quite literally, where your money is going to go. And where very, very large sums are at stake, well-choreographed site visits are becoming less reliable as a means for verifying an organization's strengths.

If the size of your proposed investment is such that it can have a significant and profound impact if applied properly, then you cannot ignore the character, commitment, candor and expertise of the trustees with whom you will entrust those funds.

There may be organizations that will balk at your requests for extensive information, attendance at a board meeting, or a board group interview. None of these requests is unreasonable; and rarely will there be a legitimate basis for refusing you.

Always keep in mind—*it's your money*! If an organization wants and deserves it, the leaders *will* accommodate your need to perform due diligence. And if the leaders won't, remember that there are many other fine charities that are deserving and share your vision—and whose leaders will have no quarrel with proving it to you.

Note: See **Appendix H: Ten Key Questions Every Board Member Should Be Able to Answer** for more information on the issues covered in this chapter.

Chapter 9

Ten Warning Signs: Where to Look for "The Bodies"

❧

There's a sucker born every minute.

—P.T. Barnum

❧

The due diligence process outlined in Chapter 8 is the most effective way to determine whether a particular charity represents a wise philanthropic investment. However, if your timeframe for making the gift does not allow for the kind of comprehensive evaluation recommended, there are "red flags" for which you should be on the lookout. Should any of these warning signs appear, think carefully about whether you should proceed with the contribution.

Warning Sign No. 1

You are discouraged or barred from a site visit or board meeting.
There is virtually no reason why someone with a legitimate

interest in a charity should be dissuaded from visiting the organization. Issues of client confidentiality may arise for charities such as substance abuse rehabilitation centers, shelters for battered women, agencies serving abused children, and the like. In those circumstances, it is usually still possible to visit common or public areas of the facility where the privacy of clients would not be compromised.

The same is true for your request to observe a board meeting. Naturally, there may be highly confidential matters on the agenda for a board meeting, such as specific personnel issues, legal actions in which the charity is involved, or discussion of a potential major gift. Offer to excuse yourself from the board meeting should any such topic arise for discussion. There should also be no hesitation on the board's part in sharing with you documents or financial reports circulated at the meeting.

There may be other rare instances when an agency is reticent to have you visit its facility, one of its service sites, or a board meeting. Listen to the charity's justification for keeping you at a distance. Does it sound reasonable? Does the nonprofit offer any alternative means for you to have an "up close and personal" experience with the organization and its leaders? Make your judgment of their motives on a case-by-case basis, but don't take a flat-out "no" for an answer on this one.

Warning Sign No. 2

Financial records are unavailable, unintelligible, or generally in disarray.

Bells and whistles should go off for you if an organization is unable or unwilling to provide you with a clear picture—in writing—of its financial position. This would generally indicate that an organization is either hiding something about their finances or is so disorganized financially that you would be foolish to invest in the charity at this time.

At the very least, there are three documents that should be readily available to you as a potential donor.

First would be a statement of the agency's financial activities for the most recently completed fiscal year. This may be in the form of a financial compilation prepared by an accountant, a fully audited financial statement prepared by an independent certified public accountant or simply a year-by-year line-item expense/revenue tally kept by the organization on an ongoing basis.

The second financial document you should be able to request is a current year operating budget—what the organization anticipates receiving and spending this year.

Lastly, any nonprofit organization with an annual budget over $25,000 is required to file a Form 990 informational tax return with the IRS each year in order to maintain its tax-exempt status. Under the law, an organization must provide this document to anyone requesting it. It lists general sources, uses, and amounts for revenues and expenditures by key category, as well as compensation received by the highest paid administrators and/or officers of the nonprofit.

Embezzlement and misappropriation of funds is not unheard of in the nonprofit sector. Often, board members are unaware of such activities because they themselves are discouraged from looking at key records or original documentation.

Out of respect for the confidentiality of information about major or anonymous donors, there really is no valid reason to hide basic financial records or data from you as a potential contributor, or from any board member.

Warning Sign No. 3

There is no written strategic or business plan for the organization.
Without a road map leading from today's position to tomorrow's destination, it's awfully difficult to make the trip without wasting time, energy, and resources (including financial resources). A sound organization will have documented—in writing—its vision, goals, and objectives. And the leaders of the organization should be able to explain to you how your contribution will be utilized to forward the plan.

Consensus is generally required before committing a plan to writing. The danger when no written plan exists is that one or more of the agency's leaders—administrators or board directors—will have varying or conflicting plans for where the organization is heading—and perhaps even how your contribution will be used. Worse yet, they have no plans at all and are waiting for your gift to inspire them to think of one.

Warning Sign No. 4

The executive director discourages you from speaking with a board member or a board member discourages you from speaking with an administrator.
    This should be another bell-ringer for you. Beware of a charity where the executive director makes a concerted effort to shield contact between the board and the outside world. Often in such cases, the executive director runs the show—the whole show—and has assembled a figurehead, rubber-stamp board that plays only a very limited role in governing the organization. That limited role generally does not include oversight of the administration and management of the charity. This vacuum is where all sorts of "funny business" can go on.

    Conversely, be cautious in supporting an organization where the board is engaged in "micromanagement." Unless the agency is purely a volunteer-run charity, the role of executive director is a very important one. This person should be aware of and responsible for the day-to-day operations of the charity. And, in most cases, the top administrator would be the one most familiar with the exact financial and service activities of the organization. When straight answers are required, the executive director is most likely to have—and to give—them. There is really no reason why board members should wish to shield you from their chief executive.

Warning Sign No. 5

Fewer than 70% of the board members have made a financial contribution to the organization within the last twelve months.
    If a charity is doing fine and valuable work, what possible reason could there be for fewer than 100% of its stewards, its trustees, to be making an annual contribution? Good question, no good

answer. This matter is covered in detail in Chapter 8. The only acceptable reason for less than 100% participation is that several trustees have only recently joined the board and simply have not had the time to write their check yet.

"Do as I say, not as I do" does not cut it when you're considering making a substantial (actually, any size) contribution to a charity. Giving to an un-giving board is like going to a fortune teller who tells you to leave all your money in a gym bag with a newt's eye and a lizard's toe and promises to transform it into unseen wealth. Unseen is right—you'll never see it again. Follow the board members' lead—hang onto your money (or find a more committed board) and let them experiment with someone else's investment.

Warning Sign No. 6

More money is spent on administration and fundraising than on programs and services.

Determining how much is being spent on overhead expenses versus service can be tough. Charities have become very concerned with keeping the appearance of non-program-related costs low. Some have become quite creative at this. Carefully review the financial documents referenced above with a pencil and scratchpad at hand. Note next to each line item whether the expense is more "program"-related (P) or "other" (O). If you are unsure of the nature of an expenditure, ask the organization's financial officer or executive director to briefly explain it. Listen for any "doublespeak." Add up the P's and O's—P's should total a lot more than the O's. Ideally, the O's would constitute between 20% and 40% of the charity's total expenditures. The lower the number the better.

Some organizations separate their fundraising financials from the rest of their budget information. This is sometimes done as a means of keeping the total fundraising expense "off the books," with only the net fundraising revenue being referenced in the overall organizational budget. For example, you might find that the annual gala cost $60,000 to mount but brought in only $15,000 for the sponsoring charity. You would probably think twice about signing on as a $25,000 "angel"—especially if a portion of the $15,000 net is going to cover organizational overhead costs.

Warning Sign No. 7

The charity is involved in a legal action.

Contribute with caution while an organization is involved in a legal dispute, particularly as the defendant. In the worst case, should the complainant prevail, the nonprofit may be forced to liquidate assets in order to satisfy a judgment, or even dissolve altogether as a charitable corporation. Your gift would have been for naught. Just defending itself against a legal action could consume substantial organizational assets.

It is always wise to inquire of a charity whether it is currently involved in any legal action, or if the board or executive director is aware of any pending or imminent legal suit. If the answer is affirmative, ask the agency whether there is an insurance policy or other mechanism in place that will protect or minimize the lawsuit's impact on the organization's financial stability.

There is one other reason to inquire about recent or current legal actions involving the charity. The nature of the matter may be such that it reflects negatively on the judgment or actions of the organization and its leadership. For example, if the matter involves financial mismanagement or malfeasance, harassment or discrimination, or self-dealing, self-interest, or conflict of interest issues, you may have some qualms about investing financially in the organization.

Of course, every dispute has two sides. Get as much information as possible before making or denying a contribution to an organization involved in a legal dispute. Better yet, you might wait until the matter is resolved before making your final determination.

Warning Sign No. 8

The organization cannot or will not provide you with the names and contact information for other or past financial supporters.

Unless a charity is brand spanking new, someone somewhere had to provide some financial support to the organization. If no one else, the charity's founders or inaugural board should have shown some level of financial commitment to the agency (see Warning Sign No. 5).

Anyone can fake a financial statement or even a list of current or past donors. It's harder to orchestrate a phone call or in-person meeting with someone who doesn't exist. Ideally, you would want to know who else has given gifts comparable in size to your own. Check with that donor to determine whether he or she felt the contribution had been well-utilized for the purpose for which it was given. Was the charity attentive in reporting on the use of the funds? Would this donor have any hesitation about contributing to the same charity in the future?

Warning Sign No. 9

Organization leaders cannot or will not reveal specific salary or other expenditure information.

Any time a charity displays a hesitation in revealing financial information to a prospective donor, *Beware*! A well-run and legitimate charity operating in the public interest as a nonprofit corporation under a privilege of tax-exemption granted by the federal government has no reason to hide financial information.

As noted in Warning Sign No. 2, salary information for the top-paid leaders is a matter of public record for charities with annual budgets over $25,000. What benefits or perks, if any, do employees or board members enjoy as a result of their service to the organization? In addition to employees, what is the organization paying key service providers, consultants, fundraisers, vendors, landlords, etc.? Do these sums represent fair market value? Are any of these parties also directors of the board, employees, relatives of directors or employees, or in some other way closely connected to the organization? The relationship is itself not an issue, as long as the financial transaction reflects the same cost or a lower cost than the agency would have paid someone else for the same service.

Warning Sign No. 10:

Your gut tells you that something is "off."

All of the axioms that you rely on in your everyday financial transactions can be applied to your consideration of a charitable gift:

"If it sounds too good to be true, it probably is."

"Where there's smoke, there's fire."

"If it looks like a duck, walks like a duck, and quacks like a duck ...."

Do not let yourself be blinded to inconsistencies, unanswered questions, or vagueness of purpose simply because you are dealing with a charitable cause whose stated mission is emotionally compelling.

Summary

The range of human needs is great. The opportunities for making the world a better place are virtually infinite. Anyone can make an organization look good on paper. As a philanthropist, take the time to do some investigating. Get to know something about the people who will be making decisions about how your money will be used. It is the single best indicator that your gift will be a sound investment.

If you have any doubt or question that your contribution to a charity might be better spent—could have a more meaningful or profound impact on your community or the world community— with another organization, listen to your instincts.

After all, there are only 649,999 other charities (roughly) in the U.S. alone to choose from.

Note: The following appendixes deal with issues covered in this chapter:

- **Appendix I: Donor Bill of Rights**
- **Appendix J: Model Standards of Practice for the Gift Planner**

Chapter 10

Attaching Strings: Negotiating Your Gift to Maximize Philanthropic Return

❦

Nothing has more strength than dire necessity.

—Euripides

❦

A s emphasized throughout this book, the true philanthropist's ultimate objective is to foster a change in the world—or in some small part of it—that will make it a better place.

Change requires resources: money, energy, time, talent, commitment, conviction, to name just a few.

Let's be perfectly frank—money drives the nonprofit sector. Good intentions remain just that if an organization—at some point—does not harness the financial resources to transform intention into action. A committed nonprofit will go to extraordinary measures to secure significant gifts. For that reason, the donor or potential donor holds an enormous amount of power in the charitable sector.

You can use your contribution to buy a table at the gala, underwrite a program, finance a portion of construction, or keep an organization afloat in times of trouble. This approach to giving, however, is tantamount to giving a hungry man a fish.

As a philanthropist, you perform a service to the nonprofit when your contribution leads or encourages the charity to grow stronger or more effective. In other words, motivate or teach the hungry man to CATCH a fish.

The simplest way to do this is to negotiate reasonable conditions on your gift that will encourage—or force—the nonprofit to operate more efficiently and serve more effectively.

Matching and Challenge Grants

One common method for maximizing the philanthropic and financial value of your gift is to structure it as a matching or challenge contribution. In other words, tie the size or timing of your gift to the organization's success in securing funding from other or new sources.

Not so many years ago, a "jewel box" of a community cultural center found itself eyeball to eyeball with the founding donor after whom the theater had been named. As it had for each of the preceding five years, the organization's board had requested a $100,000 contribution for operating expenses.

In fact, so sure was the board of its patroness's continuing support that they had already inked her anticipated $100,000 into the year's operating budget.

They were a little surprised when she asked for a luncheon meeting at her club to discuss the request. They were shocked when she took them to task for treating her family foundation as a "cash cow." She pointed out that the board had grown lazy about reaching out to the whole community both with services and for support. She scolded them for continuing to rely on a relatively small pool of donors who would eventually move away, pass away, or otherwise withdraw their support from the center.

This wise philanthropist flat-out refused their request for the $100,000. But she made them an even more lucrative offer: if and when the board and staff were able to secure a total of $100,000 from donors who had never contributed to the theater before, she would give $100,000 as well. In fact, if they secured $125,000 from new donors, she would donate $150,000 for the year!

The shock of losing the $100,000 it had counted on and the incentive of potentially bringing in a total of $275,000 that year from new donors and their patron philanthropist was *exactly* the "kick in the pants" that charity needed.

This donor was also quite savvy about how nonprofits sometimes "fudge" the data to meet funding requirements. At the time she made her offer, she requested a complete list of current and former donors. When the nonprofit had secured the target sum from new donors, the charity was to provide their names and donation amounts for comparison.

As a result of the deal negotiated by the donor, the nonprofit brought in $175,000 more than it had set as a goal in the original budget. More importantly, the charity's leaders and staff worked to attract over 300 bona fide new donors—new constituents with whom they now had a relationship on which they could build in the coming years.

And most important, in order to keep both the established and new donors committed to the nonprofit's mission, there was a renewed emphasis on developing and improving programs and services so that they truly remained relevant and responsive to the changing needs and demographics of the community.

Technical Assistance

Traditionally, nonprofits come into being when deeply committed individuals come together for the purpose of filling an unmet need. As traced in Chapter 5, the growth of the charity will eventually require a professional staff and/or a corps of volunteers knowledgeable about the many disciplines that go into running a successful organization.

With financial resources tight, most growing charities cannot afford to hire the most experienced professionals available, or even to offer comprehensive advanced training to committed volunteers.

Very often, in even the large charities, the top administrator is a former "practitioner" in the charity's service field who has risen through the ranks as the organization grew. Soon, this individual may be heading a multi-million dollar agency with little or no formal training or guidance in key management areas such as finance, human resources, strategic planning, or program evaluation.

This phenomenon is replicated through the ranks. The first fundraising staff member hired is usually one with limited experience—that's all the organization can afford. Yet as the charity develops, the fundraising goals will increase, and unless that manager gains knowledge and support in more advanced forms of fundraising, the organization will be hurt.

One of the best investments a philanthropist can make is in people—the people who manage or lead charitable organizations.

The executive director of a major children's services agency had been at the helm since being hired as the charity's first paid staff member. His importance in the community as well as in the field of children's services had grown with the organization. By virtue of his personality and long-term affiliation with the charity, he was a valuable asset to the agency.

The organization grew to several sites across a major metropolitan area, serving hundreds of children through the work of both paid social service professionals and hundreds of trained volunteers. The financial needs of the organization grew in proportion to its size and scope of service.

The executive director, never having led an operation of this size, grew frazzled and disorganized, often snapping at co-workers, colleagues, and board leaders. Large "things" started to fall through the cracks. Organizational "backslide" was imminent. Something had to change. Clearly, the executive director needed management training.

The agency's bare-bones budget could not support even a relatively modest investment in professional development for the executive director. One perceptive philanthropist, however, recognized that his charitable investment in the agency was not being fully maximized because the executive director's leadership potential was not being maximized.

This donor's next contribution came with the stipulation that a portion of his gift be allocated toward management training and an "executive coach" for the top administrator.

The board was so pleased with the results and with this innovative approach to "investing" in the agency that it subsequently solicited funds from donors specifically for improving the skills and knowledge base of key staff.

Some donors and organizations may worry about investing resources in personnel who might eventually move on and be lost to the agency. As a philanthropist, your investment in nonprofit leaders will rarely be wasted. Most of these individuals will move to other agencies where they will apply the knowledge and expertise they have gained toward other pressing community needs.

Is technical assistance equally valuable for larger charitable institutions? Absolutely! In the largest organizations, the demands of overseeing a major operation or directing a key office (for example, the Development Office of a major university or medical center) forces professional development activities or opportunities to the bottom of the priority list. It is absolutely critical to expose those leaders to innovations they might not otherwise encounter within their own institution. Using your charitable contribution to "force" leaders to step away from their home institution to gain perspective on developments in the field and changes in the service environment is an important and under-utilized model of philanthropy.

Planning Assistance: Method One

A great deal of nonprofit service is motivated and driven by hope rather than by a well-researched, well-conceived, and clearly articulated plan. Philanthropists could have a profound impact on

115

the effectiveness of the charitable sector if they simply demanded to see a plan—business, strategic, development, or other—before providing money to a charity. Providing funds to an organization without seeing a written work plan is like dropping money into a slot machine—or buying a stock without investigating its prospects.

The popular press is rarely at a loss for a head-scratching story on some charity that closed its doors or ceased operations when everything seemed "fine" just the week or month before. In most such cases, current success blinded an organization's leadership to changes just over the horizon.

There are two methods by which a philanthropist can ensure the wise and prudent use of his or her charitable investment. The first is requiring the charity to develop and present a written plan before a contribution will be considered. Nonprofit leaders—executives and trustees—are great "spinners." The same passion and creativity that inspires one to tackle the human or social condition is what propels one past the fear of talking to a potential major donor. If a charity's charismatic representative has painted a compelling verbal portrait of the organization's vision, and asks for your support, ask to see the organization's overall written strategic plan. It's as simple as that. Unless there is a solid written plan, your proposed investment is at risk.

A regional cultural organization turned to one of America's most prominent charitable donors and, on the strength of a personal relationship, a major gift toward new construction was secured. The organization, however, had not finalized an architectural or building plan, nor had it projected revenues or expenditures related to this major project. Fundraising moved at a snail's pace while construction plans (and costs) escalated. Usage and programming plans changed dramatically over the years as the building project dragged on, causing serious embarrassment for the charity. More than one early donor had contributed specifically for a building element or exhibit that was no longer part of the final plan!

Moreover, the continually changing plan caused prospective donors to hesitate in both the timing and the size of their contributions.

The new institution was finally completed, and it opened to great fanfare and success. But at what cost of additional time, money, and good will? No lead donor, early on, had insisted on seeing a comprehensive, detailed, fundable plan.

In a different case, a philanthropist chose to use the power of his potential contribution to strengthen the *organization* that sought his support—in addition to supporting its *project*.

A community arts entity preparing to undertake a capital campaign approached a locally based celebrity figure who had been supportive of its efforts in the past. The representatives were hoping for at least an indication that a major gift would be forthcoming toward the project once announced.

This experienced philanthropist and businessman made it clear that he would be happy to discuss the project once it was past the "concept" stage and there was a thorough, written business plan that he could examine.

The charity, recognizing the importance of this gentleman's support, undertook a detailed planning process, addressing every aspect of the project from construction funding to budget, program, and usage projections for the next several years. This effort proved tremendously useful to the organization, resulting in a detailed "roadmap" that will keep the charity on a steady course through a period of substantial transformation over the next five years.

As an added benefit, the organization was far better positioned to solicit major gifts for its capital campaign than it otherwise would have been, and donors responded with larger gifts than were anticipated.

This organization admits it would not have spent the time or effort to develop a detailed plan had that not been a condition laid down by the philanthropist.

Planning Assistance: Method Two

The second method a philanthropist can employ to encourage sound and solid planning is to pay for or provide a specialist or professional to lead the charity through a planning process.

A small independent elementary school with a rigorous yet creative curriculum had been struggling to establish itself for years. The founding donor subsidized the school's operating costs while his children were enrolled. As they moved up to high school, his funding focus shifted to the institutions his children were now attending. From a high enrollment of 50, the school had slipped to 29 students over its ten-year history.

Late one spring, recognizing that his past investment in the school would be a loss if he did not do something to ensure the school's continued existence, the philanthropist offered to pay for the expense of a strategic planning consultant if the board would commit to engage in the planning process. He let the board know he thought it would take working evenings and weekends if they were to save and grow the school by fall. He also made it clear that if they were not interested in his offer, his future support could not be ensured.

By bringing in a professional to lead the planning process, the board was able to accomplish in six months what it had been struggling to do for ten years. The members had simply lacked the expertise—and the resources to bring in the expertise—to develop a working plan, an action plan.

In six months, enrollment went from 29 to 90. One year later, it was at 149, and the board was negotiating with the local public school district to lease a closed school site. Two years later, the student body approached three hundred.

The million-dollars-plus that the founding philanthropist had poured into operations over the ten years had a smaller impact on the children of the community than the several thousand dollars spent on providing the school with planning assistance.

Multi-Year Gifts

Another very effective means for motivating a charity to develop a stronger infrastructure is to spread your contribution over a period of several quarters or years. Assign benchmarks of financial, administrative, or program performance; development of written strategic, evaluation, or fund development plans; professional development for staff and administration; or other verifiable or quantifiable actions designated to improve the organization's operation or governance.

Be clear about your expectations for both the use of your investment and the measures by which you will determine whether you will release the next installment of your contribution.

It is interesting to note that there is a tremendous pool of talented administrators in the nonprofit sector. As a group, they are generally more effective in their role as administrators than most board directors are as trustees.

It is not unusual for an executive director to see what an organization needs to do in order to grow, improve, or become more "fundable." Directors run into an obstacle, however, when trying to lead the board to that same understanding.

As a philanthropist, you have enormous power to influence charities to "do the right thing." And often, one of your strongest allies will be the top administrator. By placing conditions on your gift, by phasing your gift to "reward" positive change and development on the part of the organization—as well as to fund worthy programs and services—you multiply the value of your contribution.

Summary

❧
Advice is seldom welcome,
and those who want it the most
always like it the least.
—*Lord Chesterfield*
❧

It cannot be emphasized enough that when donors speak, the board listens. In fact, you would be surprised by how many nonprofit leaders—behind closed doors—are unashamedly amused by the large gifts simply handed over without investigation or condition.

Many donors wonder whether it is "fair" to place conditions on their gift. It is "fair" to the extent that, presumably, those conditions are intended to strengthen the organization's ability to serve as well and as effectively as possible.

In that respect, both the philanthropist and the charity share the same objective. A strong charity will not only welcome your input, but will even seek it.

Do not diminish your ability or power to provoke constructive change in the world by simply writing a check to a charity. Explore all avenues for increasing the value and return on your investment.

As a philanthropist you can change the world *and* strengthen the nonprofit sector, if you *only* take the opportunity.

Part Four

Going Beyond
the Gift

Chapter 11

Tracking Your Philanthropic Investments and Measuring Their Performance

❧

We need above all to know about changes;
no one wants or needs to be reminded 16 hours a day
that his shoes are on.

—David Hubel

❧

I f you have carefully followed the steps and tips shared in this book for selecting and evaluating a charity for your philanthropic investment, tracking the impact of your donation will be fairly straightforward.

The most important rule is to be sure and do follow up on your investment. Charities change, usually when their leadership changes. Administrators are fired or leave, trustees rotate off the board, and new directors come on to govern. Financial projections can miss, causing priorities to be realigned.

Typically, donors receive an acknowledgment for their gift and, eventually, a report on how their gift was utilized to accomplish the success it was expected to fund—in David Hubel's words, reminding us that "(their) shoes are on." This pro forma report, however, is not an adequate means for you to determine whether your investment "paid off," or even if it was used per your intentions.

Be aware that many nonprofits, even among the largest, will assume that if the donor does not keep in touch about their gift, the charity has some leeway about how to use it if conditions change.

In fact, if at the time you transmit your gift, you do not specify the purpose for which it is to be used, many charities will assume it is theirs to do with as they please. This can be true even if your gift was solicited on the basis of supporting some specific need or program.

Ross Perot, a seasoned donor who has contributed tens of millions to charity, has no hesitation in asking for his money back if the organization hasn't spent it as agreed. And neither should you.

Prepare a Contract

Tracking your gift begins prior to the conveyance of funds or assets. Be sure to place in writing your understanding of how—exactly—the contribution will be used. Articulate any conditions clearly, and specify how and by when the charity is to verify that it has met those conditions. Make it clear that the charity must notify you in the event that it is unable—for any reason—to apply your donation in the manner intended. That way, it remains in your power to determine whether a different usage of your funds by that charity would still accomplish your philanthropic objectives.

Detours of fund do happen. Not long ago, it was revealed that a very prestigious and internationally recognized East Coast university had accepted a $3 million pledge to establish a chair in Holocaust studies. Three years later, with the school unable to agree on a candidate to fill the position, a substantial portion of the gift was quietly reapportioned to the university's medical school.

Once you have laid out the "contract" on which your gift will be based, send two copies of this agreement to the nonprofit, and ask the director to sign and return both copies to you. Send one copy of the fully executed agreement back to the charity along with your contribution or donation instrument.

Maintain a Personal Connection

Your schedule permitting, continue to track the organization's progress and activities using the same techniques and methods used to assess the charity originally: for example, make site visits, ask for updated financial records, visit a board meeting, or take a few trustees to breakfast or lunch.

Ask specifically about the application of your funds. Have they been expended, and if so, how? Is your gift having, overall, the impact you had envisioned?

If you are unable to maintain contact personally, consider using a consultant or perhaps a family member to maintain the contact on your behalf.

Verify the Impact of Your Investment

Ask that the executive director or program director send you a *letter* once per quarter briefly updating you on the progress being made in the program, service, or operational area that you are supporting.

Let them know that you are not looking for a *report*. A report is a document of length and detail that is usually designed to obscure both the excitement and problems that are being encountered. You truly want the charity to view you as a partner in its work, and partnerships are successful only when all parties can be candid with one another.

Encourage the organization to share information with you

about any "glitches" that come up. Two heads are better than one. You may have information, experience, or resources that would be of use to the nonprofit in overcoming an unexpected challenge.

Share the Wealth

❦

*The only thing one can do with good advice is to
pass it on. It is never of any use to oneself.*
—Oscar Wilde

❦

As you develop a focus for your philanthropy, you will become aware of other organizations, innovations, experiments, and successes in your field of focus. Some of these innovations and successes will be a direct result of the investment you made in a program or charity. Others you will learn of as you investigate giving opportunities.

Do not let this knowledge be wasted! Share the contacts you have made. Allow yourself to be a networking agent among the many charities you will encounter on your philanthropic journey that can benefit from one another's work.

In recent years, there has been a trend among funders to be more generous with organizations involved in a collaborative effort with other charities. The original thinking was that collaboration and joint activities could reduce overhead expenses and increase service. Research has shown, however, that although collaborative partnerships between nonprofits may improve service, overall costs do not significantly come down.

A more powerful form of "collaboration" is the linking of people—innovators who share a common goal, but who have perhaps discovered different routes to attain that goal.

As a proactive philanthropist, your growing circle of contacts in the charitable sector will become one of the most valuable assets you can share.

Encourage the beneficiaries of your investment to develop a

vision and a broadened perspective on their work through observing and experiencing the work of other agencies with similar goals. Help them identify those agencies from your growing list of contacts.

And when your investment has helped establish or improve an innovative, effective program, support the nonprofit in any effort to publicize that success and its methodologies. Other agencies in other communities—or even countries—can learn from the successes of the charity you have supported, and may even choose to replicate it. Once again, your investment has multiplied!

Summary

Sending the check, signing a trust, or conveying the stock certificate is where your philanthropic investment begins. With that act, you enter into a partnership with the charitable organization—a partnership forged to change the world.

As with any partnership, the most successful are those in which all partners are encouraged to be candid with one another as they progress toward their mutual goal.

Encourage your nonprofit partners to utilize you as more than just a "financial backer." Your experience, contacts, and intentions are valuable resources from which they might benefit—and from which the value of your investment will deepen.

Chapter 12

*Now That **You're** a Philanthropist...*

❦
Community is like a ship;
everyone ought to be prepared to take the helm.
—Henrik Ibsen
❦

Raising Community Awareness

here is an adage among charitable fundraisers that women take far longer than men in deciding to give, but when they do, they bring ten friends along with them.

Would that every philanthropist brought along ten friends!

Philanthropy, vision, a desire to change the world—or even the life of just one person we don't know—are still not easy topics for the cocktail circuit. "Philanthropy" is something most of us just don't talk about. Even among philanthropists! In fact, religion and politics enjoy a warmer welcome in conversation than does talk of philanthropy.

There is one more very powerful means by which you can dramatically increase the value and return on your philanthropy.

Talk about it.

Engage others to think critically about community, about need, about change. Be willing to share stories of the vision that you have for a better world.

There is no requirement to talk about the dollars. Talk about the journey: how you came to your personal philanthropic focus, how you chose a community in which to make your mark, what you learned through "sleuthing."

Invite others to walk the walk with you—literally. Whether on a site visit, trustee interview, or a chat with a charitable administrator, draw others into this world with you. Invite them into that world of philanthropy that labors on behind the galas, golf tournaments, and ribbon-cuttings.

Ask the question, "What is the most satisfying giving experience you've enjoyed in your life?" It a wonderful place for the discussion to start.

Teaching Philanthropy at Home

❦

*Children have never been very good
at listening to their elders,
but they have never failed to imitate them.*
—*William Wordsworth*

❦

We all realize that our children are the future. What the world becomes will be determined in large measure by the adults into which our children will grow.

Do not miss the opportunity to teach your children to be philanthropists, but not the kind who make large contributions in exchange for visibility or social position.

Teach them to be the kind of philanthropist motivated by the love of all humanity. Teach them to envision a world that is a better place for all. Show them how to invest not only for the benefit of the family, but for the benefit of the global family.

☙

There is always one moment in childhood
when the door opens and lets the future in.
—Graham Greene

☙

Create an environment in your home that invites your children to "open doors." Imagination and vision are very close cousins— and children are already born with imagination. Lead them to that next step. Show your children that a vision can become reality— all it requires is a plan and an application of resources.

Entrust your children with the power (and some money!) to make philanthropic investments. Let their contributions be guided by a personal vision. Encourage them in the selection of a giving focus, and gently steer them in the process of seeking organizations with a similar focus.

Teach your children the difference between "giving," "charity," and "philanthropy."

Give them the freedom to make dumb giving choices—and doubly support their wisely made ones. Invite them to participate in your own philanthropic journey, first as observers and eventually as partners.

If we are vigilant in raising our children as lovers of mankind, as givers toward the effort to make the world a better place, we will have made the greatest philanthropic investment of our lifetime.

☙

P.S. And don't forget Vincent Astor's admonitionalong the way:
"(Have) a hell of a lot of fun ..."!

Part Five

Appendices

General Fields of Nonprofit Endeavor

Arts, Culture, and Humanities

Educational Institutions and Related Activities

Environmental Quality, Protection, and Beautification

Animal-Related Health—General and Rehabilitative

Mental Health, Crisis Intervention

Disease, Disorders, Medical Disciplines

Medical Research

Crime, Legal-Related

Employment, Job-Related

Food, Agriculture, and Nutrition

Housing, Shelter

Public Safety, Disaster Preparedness, and Relief

Recreation, Sports, Leisure, Athletics

Youth Development

Human Services

International, Foreign Affairs, and National Security

Civil Rights, Social Action, Advocacy

Community Improvement, Capacity Building

Science and Technology Research Institutes, Services

Social Science Research Institutes, Services

Religion-Related, Spiritual Development

Technical Assistance Services

Public Policy Research and Analysis

Policy Reform

Ethics

Fund Raising and/or Fund Distribution (e.g., United Way)

Equal Opportunity and Access

Information and Referral Services

Public Education (Increasing Public Awareness)

Volunteer Bureaus

Nonprofit Diagnostic Review

Developed by Rafferty Consulting Group, © 1991.

This simple tool was developed as a means for quickly assessing the general "health" of a nonprofit organization and for helping determine its position within the lifecycle of organizational development.

The Diagnostic Review can be compared to the health-check booth you might find at a shopping mall. Just as the health-check only points to signs that suggest a deeper investigation is warranted (for example, blood pressure and pulse are high, or there is a decrease in hearing acuity), the Diagnostic Review has been developed for both nonprofit leaders and prospective donors to assess whether there are areas of function or operation that should be investigated more closely.

Directions

For each question below, select the answer that is most accurate, and fill in the corresponding point value in the blank space to the right of the question. Once all questions have been answered, total the points. Locate the total on the assessment scale at the end of the Diagnostic Review.

Mission

1. When was your organization's mission statement
   last rewritten or updated?   ____
   Within the last 6 months   3
   6 months to 1 year ago   2
   1 year to 2 years ago   1
   More than 2 years ago   0

2. How long is your mission statement?   ____
   Two paragraphs   3
   One paragraph   2
   Three paragraphs   1
   Longer than three paragraphs   0

3. Would you characterize your written mission
   statement as: ____
   Dynamic, passionate and accurate 3
   Very accurate   2
   Unclear   1
   Indistinguishable from that of
   similar organizations   0

Planning

4. When did your organization last undertake a
   formal planning process?   ____
   Within the last 6 months   3
   6 months to 1 year ago   2
   1 year to 2 years ago   1
   More than 2 years ago   0

5. Has your organization detailed a long-term or
   strategic plan in writing?   ____
   Yes   3
   "Somewhat"   1
   No   0

6. Who are the primary participants in your
    organization's formal planning process?   ____
        Board and Staff and Others   3
        Both Board AND Staff   2
        Either Board OR Staff   1
        No formal planning process   0

Program

7. When did your organization's program/activities last
    undergo a substantial change, addition, or deletion? ____
        0 to 6 months ago   3
        6 months to 1 year ago   2
        1 year to 2 years ago   1
        More than 2 years ago   0

8. How would you characterize your organization's
    program compared to those of organizations
    similar in mission, size and budget?   ____
        Ours is a model for others   3
        Ours has some "catching up" to do   2
        Ours is of a better quality than most   1
        We don't compare our program to others/
            It is just like that of others   0

9. Does your organization participate in any "strategic
    partnership" activities with other private or public
    organizations?   ____
        Yes   3
        We are in the process of exploring
            a strategic partnership   2
        No   1
        What is a "strategic partnership"
            activity?   0

Fund Development

10. In the last completed fiscal year, did your donated
    funds (unearned revenue): _____

Increase over the previous year?	3
Remain level with the previous year?	2
Decrease from the previous year?	1
Don't know/Depends on how you mean that	0

11. In the current fiscal year, are your donated funds
    (unearned revenue) _____

Increasing over last year?	3
Remaining level with last year?	2
Decreasing from last year?	1
Don't know yet	0

12. Does your organization have a written fund
    development master plan? _____

Yes	3
"Somewhat"	2
No	1
What is a "fund development master plan"?	0

13. What is your organization's main source for
    donated funds (unearned revenue)? _____

Annual campaign and corporate foundation.	3
Annual campaign	2
Select major donors	1
Special events	0

14. What percentage of donor turnover does your organization
    experience each year? _____

10%–20%	3
30%	2
40%–90%	1
0% or 100%	0

Volunteerism

15. What is the ratio of very active non-Board
    volunteers to Board+Senior Administrators?   ___
        4 V : 1 B+A   3
        2 V : 1 B+A   2
        1 V : 1 B+A   1
        Less than 1:1   0

16. Is volunteerism at your organization   ___
        Vigorously encouraged and
           proactively sought?   3
        Invited ?   2
        Suggested?   1
        Required/Ignored?   0

17. Are volunteers in your organization   ___
        Formally recognized and rewarded?   3
        Formally recognized?   2
        Rewarded?   1
        Neither   0

Public/Community Relations

18. Who within your organization has primary
    responsibilityfor communicating with the press,
    other media, and the local community?   ___
        Public/Community Relations
           Staff Officer   3
        Volunteer   2
        Executive Director   1
        Various/No one individual   0

19. How often is the community at large invited into
    your organization's facility?   ___
        More than once a year   3
        At least once a year   2
        Rarely   1
        Never   0

20. When was the last time your organization had a
    significant mention in the local or general media? ____
Within the last 60 days	3
60 to 90 days ago	2
90 days to 6 months ago	1
More than 6 months ago	0

21. When was the last time your organization had a significant
    mention in a professional or trade publication? ____
Within the last 60 days	3
60 to 90 days ago	2
90 days to 6 months ago	1
More than 6 months ago	0

22. Which of the following has the highest recognition
    factor in your community? ____
The organization's name	3
The name of one of the organization's programs	2
Board President or a Board Member	1
Executive Director	0

Board

23. What percentage of the Board directorship is in
    attendance at the average Board meeting? ____
90%–100%	3
75%–90%	2
50%–75%	1
Less than 50%	0

24. Is there a formal written Board policy or handbook
    that is given to each Board member specifically
    outlining his or her role and responsibilities? ____
Yes	3
No	0

25. Is there a formal Board nomination/election
    process that occurs on a regularly scheduled
    (annual/bi-annual) basis?   _____
Yes	3
"Somewhat"	1
No	0

26. What do your organization's Board members understand
    and act on as their primary responsibility?   _____
Fund development	3
Policy	2
Operations	1
Attending Board meetings	0

27. How often does your Board conduct a one- to
    two-day retreat   _____
Annually	3
Every two years	2
No regular schedule, but it does occur when need arises	1
Never	0

28. In your opinion, what percentage of the Board
    membership is actively involved in the
    stewardship of your organization?   _____
90%–100%	3
75%–90%	2
50%–75%	1
Less than 50%	0

Administration

29. How would you characterize the effectiveness of
    your organization's administrative team?   _____
Very strong, well-balanced team	3
Collection of talented professionals	2
Uneven	1
"One man band" (Executive Director)	0

30. How would you characterize the balance of
    executive power in your organization?   ____
        Board & Administration in equilibrium   3
        Executive Director defers to Board   2
        Board defers to Executive Director   1
        Who's running the show?   0

31. How are key administrators encouraged to further
    their professional development?   ____
        Organization requires professional
            development and pays for it   3
        Organization recognizes and rewards
            professional development   2
        Organization is not opposed to
            professional development   1
        Organization discourages/penalizes
            professional development   0

Staff

32. How would you characterize the staff turnover
    rate at your organization?   ____
        Low turnover   3
        Turnover rate fluctuates widely   2
        High turnover   1
        Very high turnover/No turnover   0

33. How frequently do most staff members participate
    in professional development activities at the
    organization's expense?   ____
        Often   3
        Occasionally   2
        Extremely rarely   1
        Never   0

34. Are staff members encouraged to advance within
    the organization?   ____
        Very strongly encouraged; organization is
          creative in accommodating talent   3
        Each staff member is on an
          advancement track   2
        Somewhat encouraged; there is little
          room for advancement   1
        Not at all/Advancement not addressed   0

35. How would you characterize your staff?   ____
        Creative, energetic, committed   3
        Competent   2
        Marking time   1
        Disgruntled   0

Facilities

36. Is there a reserve fund set aside for capital
    improvements, major repairs, deferred
    maintenance?   ____
        Yes   3
        Yes, but not adequate   2
        No, but planning one   1
        No   0

37. When did your organization's facility last have
    a fresh coat of paint?   ____
        Within the last 2 years   3
        Within the last 4 years   2
        Within the last 6 years   1
        More than 6 years ago   0

38. How would you characterize your facility in general? ____
        Plenty of space/Room to grow   3
        Adequate   2
        Getting a little tight   1
        Very cramped/Limits our program   0

Finance

39. Last fiscal year, our organization: ____
        Ended the year in the black   3
        Broke even   2
        Ended the year in the red   1
        Don't know/Depends on how
           you look at it   0

40. Based on current projections, does your organization expect to finish the current fiscal year ____
        In the black?   3
        Breaking even?   2
        In the red?   1
        Don't know/Depends on
           how you look at it   0

41. Which financial documents are reviewed at every Board meeting? ____
        Budget Variance to Date,
        Cash Flow and Earned Income   3
        Budget Variance to Date   2
        Varies   1
        Financial documents are rarely
           reviewed at Board meetings   0

Total Score ____

Nonprofit Diagnostic Review Scoring Guide

100–123 Healthy, vibrant organization
    Peaking within the Maintenance/Mature stage or the Creative stage.

82–99 Very strong organization, needing continued application of energy and resources
    Entering the Maintenance/Mature stage or transitioning from Renewal into Maturity.

60–81 Organization has peaked, needs additional energy
and resources in order to re-vitalize
In the late (downswing) stage of Maintenance/
Maturity or transitioning into Renewal.

41–59 Organization is exhibiting symptoms of hardship
or decline and requires serious attention
A critical transition point has been passed without
necessary organizational adjustments.

0–40 Organization is in serious and advanced stage of
decline, facing threat of closure
Without immediate application of energy and
resources—most probably under new leadership—the
organization will fail.

For instructions on how to use the Nonprofit Diagnostic Review for
a more advanced organizational assessment, please contact:

Rafferty Consulting Group
(760) 776-9606
Fax (760) 776-9608
e-mail: raffcons@ix.netcom.com

Organizations, Publications, and Web Sites Serving Philanthropists

Organizations

The Council of Foundations

The Council offers a comprehensive range of services and resource for foundations. It also serves members by foundation type, including Family Foundations, Community Foundations, and Corporate Foundations, with conferences, publications and resources available to serve the unique needs of each group.
1828 L Street, Suite 300
Washington, DC 20036 USA
Ph: (202) 466-6512
Fax: (202) 466-5722
http://www.cof.org

The National Center for Family Philanthropy

Through research, educational materials, and programs, the National Center offers donors, families, and those who advise them both the encouragement and the expertise needed to create

and sustain their charitable giving while informing the larger public of the value of private philanthropy.
1220 19th Street, N.W., Suite 804
Washington, DC 20036 USA
Ph: (202) 293-3424
Fax: (202) 293-3395
http://www.ncfp.org

Independent Sector
A nonprofit coalition of over 850 corporate, foundation, and voluntary organizations. Provides a variety of publications, meetings, and other resources aimed at explaining and protecting the operations of the independent sector, and working to encourage philanthropy, volunteering, not-for-profit initiative, and citizen action that help better serve people and communities.
1828 L Street, N.W.
Washington, DC 20036 USA
Ph: (202) 223-8100
Fax: (202) 416-0580
http://www.indepsec.org

The Philanthropy Roundtable
The Philanthropy Roundtable is a national association of individual donors, corporate giving representatives, foundation staff and trustees, and trust and estate officers. The Roundtable is founded on the principle that voluntary private action offers the best means of addressing many of society's needs, and that a vibrant private sector is critical to creating the wealth that makes philanthropy possible.
1150 17th Street, NW Suite 503
Washington, DC 20036 USA
Ph: (202) 822-8333
Fax: (202) 822-8325
http://www.philanthropyroundtable.org

The Forum of Regional Associations of Grantmakers (RAGs)
The Forum of RAG's mission is to promote philanthropy by inspiring and enhancing the leadership and capacity of RAGs and their members in promoting the public good.

1828 L Street, NW, Suite 300
Washington, DC 20036-5168 USA
Ph: (202) 467-0472
Fax: (202) 466-5722
http://www.rag.org

The Foundation Center
The mission of the Foundation Center is to foster public under-standing of the foundation field by collecting, organizing, analyzing, and disseminating information on foundations, corporate giving, and related subjects. Our audiences include grantseekers, grant-makers, researchers, policymakers, the media, and the general public.
79 Fifth Avenue/16th Street
New York, NY 10003-3076 USA
Ph: (212) 620-4230 or (800) 424-9836
Fax: (212) 807-3677
http://www.fdncenter.org

The Impact Project
A small member-supported nonprofit established in 1991 whose mission is to encourage people with wealth to significantly con-tribute their money and talents toward creating a more sustainable and just world.
2244 Alder St.
Eugene, OR 97405 USA
Ph: (541) 343-2420
Fax: (541) 343-6956
http://www.efn.org/~impact

National Charities Information Bureau
NCIB's mission is to promote informed giving and to enable more contributors to make sound giving decisions. NCIB believes that donors are entitled to accurate information about the charitable organizations that seek their support. NCIB also believes that well-informed givers will ask questions and make judgments that will lead to an improved level of performance by charitable organizations.
19 Union Square West
New York, NY 10003 USA
Ph: (212) 929-6300
Fax: (212) 463-7083
http://www.give.org

148

Women's Philanthropy Institute

This is a nonprofit educational institute governed by women, which joins philanthropists, volunteers, and professional funders to educate and empower women as philanthropists, donators, and volunteers. There is an online newsletter, information about a speakers bureau, and relevant links.
1605 Monroe Street, Suite 105
Madison, WI 53711 USA
Ph: (608) 286-0980
Fax: (608) 286-0978
http://www.women-philanthropy.org

National Network of Grantmakers

NNG is a membership association of funders committed to supporting progressive social change. NNG is committed to the goal of increasing resources, financial and otherwise, to organizations working for social and economic justice. Our members are individual donors, foundation staff, board, and grantmaking committee members.
San Diego Office:
1717 Kettner Blvd. Suite 110
San Diego, CA 92101 USA
Ph: (619) 231-1348
Fax: (619) 231-1349
Atlanta Office:
547 Ponce de Leon, Suite 100
Atlanta, GA 30308 USA
Ph: (404) 874-6703
Fax: (404) 874-0296
http://www.nng.org

Publications

The Chronicle of Philanthropy

The Chronicle of Philanthropy is the newspaper of the nonprofit world. Published every other week, it is the primary news source for charity leaders, fund raisers, grant makers, and other people involved in the philanthropic enterprise.

1255 23rd Street, N.W.
Washington, DC 20037 USA
Ph: (800) 728-2819 from the United States or
Ph: (740) 382-3322 from other countries
http://www.philanthropy.com

Foundation News and Commentary
Published bimonthly by the Council on Foundations, Inc.
1828 L. Street NW, Suite 300
Washington, DC 20036 USA
Ph: (202) 466-6512
Fax: (202 223-6292
http://www.cof.org

Philanthropy
Quarterly publication of The Philanthropy Roundtable.
1150 17th Street NW, Suite 503
Washington, DC 20036 USA
Ph: (202) 822-8333
Fax: (202) 822-8325
http://www.philanthropyroundtable.org

The Wise Giving Guide
The conclusions of NCIB reports are summarized in their quarterly publication, *The Wise Giving Guide*, which also lists close to 400 national organizations in a *Quick Reference Guide*. *The Wise Giving Guide* indicates whether an organization meets NCIB Standards and, if not, which ones it does not meet, and also contains articles on current issues in the charitable sector.
19 Union Square West
New York, NY 10003 USA
Ph: (212) 929-6300
Fax: (212) 463-7083
http://www.give.org

More Than Money
Quarterly publication of the Impact Project.
2244 Alder St.
Eugene, OR 97405 USA
Ph: (541) 343 -2420
Fax: (541) 343 -6956
http://www.efn.org/~impact

Web Sites Focused on Philanthropy

American Philanthropy Review

A rich site featuring over a dozen e-mail discussion forums on topics including the law as it relates to the charitable and philanthropic sectors, planned giving, governance, and ethics with over 20,000 experts and participants from around the globe. The site also includes book reviews, searchable archives, a Consultants Registry, Conference and Events listings, and an online bookstore.
http://www.charitychannel.com/

Philanthropy News Network

Host site for *Philanthropy Journal Online*, a daily Web-based news publication focusing on the nonprofit and philanthropic sectors, as well as *Philanthropy Journal Alert*, highlights from *Philanthropy Journal Online* delivered to your e-mail address free twice weekly.
http://www.pj.org

GuideStar

This 'donor's guide to the nonprofit university' includes a news service with philanthropic abstracts from the Lexis-Nexis service, information on the finances and programs of over 600,000 U.S. nonprofit organizations and charities, resources for donors and volunteers, plus cartoons, tips on the nonprofit sector, and links to other resources. This site will also allow you access to a searchable database of IRS records for all 501(c)(3) nonprofit organizations.
http://www2.guidestar.org

Charity Village

An excellent source of news, information, nonprofit resources, and discussions for the Canadian nonprofit community, with English and French paths, an online newsletter, bulletin boards, career opportunities, in-kind exchanges of goods and services, coming events, an online bookstore, and links to related sites.
http://www.charityvillage.com

NGONet

NGONet provides information to, for, and about non-governmental organizations (NGOs) active in Central and Eastern Europe. It

provides resources for funders, grantseekers, organizations look-ing for project partners, and job seekers, as well as an online library and downloadable grant applications, grant guidelines, a calendar of events, training programs, news, and a bulletin board.
http://www.ngonet.org

Internal Revenue Service (IRS)
This IRS site offers state-by-state downloadable files of tax-exempt organizations.
http://www.irs.ustreas.gov/prod/tax_stats/soi/ex_imf.html

Comprehensive Directory of Grantmaking Associations

Regional Associations of Grantmakers (U.S.)

Northern California Grantmakers
116 New Montgomery Street, Suite 742
San Francisco, CA 94105
Ph: (415) 777-5761
Fax: (415) 777-1714

Donors Forum of Wisconsin
117 West Boundary Road
Mequon, WI 53092
Ph: (414) 241-3973
Fax: (414) 241-3924

Donors Forum, Inc.
600 Brickell Avenue, Suite 206K
Miami, FL 33131
Ph: (305) 371-7944
Fax: (305) 371-2080

Northern New Mexico Grantmakers
P.O. Box 9280
Santa Fe, NM 87504-9280
Ph: (505) 995-0933
Fax: (505) 989-4533

NY Regional Association of Grantmakers
505 Eighth Avenue, Suite 1805
New York, NY 10018
Ph: (212) 714-0699
Fax: (212) 239-2075
http://www.nyrag.org

Southern California Association for Philanthropy
315 West Ninth Street, Suite 1000
Los Angeles, CA 90015-4210
Ph: (213) 489-7307
Fax: (213) 489-7320
http://www.scap.org

Conference of Southwest Foundations
3102 Maple Avenue, Suite 260
Dallas, TX 75201
Ph: (214) 740-1787
Fax: (214) 740-1790
http://www.rag.org/csf/csfindex.html

Rochester Grantmakers Forum
55 St. Paul Street
Rochester, NY 14604
Ph: (716) 232-2380
Fax: (716) 232-8413

Washington Regional Association of Grantmakers
1400 16th Street NW, Suite 430
Washington, DC 20036
Ph: (202) 939-3440
Fax: (202) 939-3442

Metropolitan Association for Philanthropy
One Metropolitan Square
211 N. Broadway, Suite 1295
St. Louis, MO 63102
Ph: (314) 621-6220
Fax: (314) 621-6224
http://www.mapstl.org

Council of Michigan Foundations
One South Harbor Avenue, Suite 3
PO Box 599
Grand Haven, MI 49417
Ph: (616) 842-7080
Fax: (616) 842-1760
http://www.cmif.org

Pacific Northwest Grantmakers Forum
1305 4th Avenue, Suite 214
Seattle, WA 98101
Ph: (206) 624-9899
Fax: (206) 624-9857

Southeastern Council of Foundations
50 Hurt Plaza, Suite 350
Atlanta, GA 30303
Ph: (404) 524-0911
Fax: (404) 523-5116
http://www.sccf.org

Donors Forum of Chicago
208 South LaSalle Street, Suite 740
Chicago, IL 60604
Ph: (312) 578-0090
Fax: (312) 578-0103
http://www.donorsforum.org

Delaware Valley Grantmakers
230 South Broad Street, Suite 4C
Philadelphia, PA 19102
Ph: (215) 790-9700
Fax: (215) 790-9704
http://www.dvg.org

Indiana Donors Alliance
32 East Washington Street, #1100
Indianapolis, IN 46204-3529
Ph: (317) 630-5200
Fax: (317) 630-5210
http://www.indonors.com

Association of Baltimore Area Grantmakers
2 East Read Street, 8th Floor
Baltimore, MD 21202
Ph: (410) 727-1205
Fax: (410)727-7177
http://www.rag.org/abag

Grantmakers of Western Pennsylvania
650 Smithfield Street, Suite 240
Pittsburgh, PA 15222
Ph: (412) 471-6488
Fax: (412) 232-3115
http://www.lm.com/~gwp

Associated Grantmakers of Massachusetts, Inc.
294 Washington Street, Suite 840
Boston, MA 02108
Ph: (617) 426-2606
Fax: (617) 426-2849
http://www.agmconnect.org

Minnesota Council on Foundations
800 Baker Building
706 2nd Avenue South
Minneapolis, MN 55402-3008
Ph: (612) 338-1989
Fax: (612) 337-5089
http://www.mcf.org

The Clearinghouse for Midcontinent Foundations
PO Box 22680
Kansas City, MO 64110
Ph: (816) 235-1176, (816) 235-2342
Fax: (816) 235-1169

The Connecticut Council for Philanthropy
85 Gillett Street
Hartford, CT 06105
Ph: (860) 525-5585
Fax: (860) 525-0436
http://ctphilanthropy.org

Council of New Jersey Grantmakers
c/o Seton Hall University
School of Public Service
400 South Orange Avenue
South Orange, NJ 07079
Ph: (973) 761-5003
Fax: (973) 761-5060

Donors Forum of Ohio
16 East Broad Street, Suite 800
Columbus, OH 43215
Ph: (614) 224-1344
Fax: (614) 224-1388

San Diego Grantmakers
c/o Jacobs Center for Nonprofit Innovation
PO Box 740650
San Diego, CA 92174-0650
Ph: (619) 527-6161
Fax: (619) 527-6162

Grantmakers Forum
1422 Euclid Avenue, Suite 1370
Cleveland, OH 44115-2001
Ph: (216) 861-6223
Fax: (216) 861-6335

Other Regional Associations of Grantmakers (U.S.)

These organizations provide similar services to area grantmakers, but are not members of the Forum of RAGs of the United States.

Arizona Grantmakers Forum
c/o Wallace Foundation
2122 East Highland Avenue, Suite 400
Scottsdale, AZ 85016
Ph: (602) 381-1400
Fax: (602) 381-1575

Central Iowa Contributions Consortium
Principal Financial Group
711 High Street
Des Moines, IA 50309
Ph: (515) 247-5111

Charlotte Area Donors Forum
P.O. Box 34769
Charlotte, NC 28234-4769
Ph: (704) 376-9541
Fax: (704) 376-9541

Colorado Association of Foundations
455 Sherman, Suite 220
Denver, CO 80203
Ph: (303) 778-7587
Fax: (303) 778-0124

Corporate Community Relations Network
1800 Center Street
Camp Hill, PA 17089
Ph: (717) 763-6207
Fax: (717) 760-9645

Donors Forum of Central Florida
P.O. Box 1967
Winter Park, FL 32790-1967
Ph: (407) 647-4322
Fax: (407) 647-7716

Donors Forum of Chattanooga
1701 Sun Trust Bank Building
736 Market Street
Chattanooga, TN 37402
Ph: (423) 265-0586
Fax: (423) 265-0587

Donors Forum of Metro Louisville
c/o Robert W. Lanum, President
Stites & Harbison
PO Box 946
Jeffersonville, IN 47131
Ph: (812) 282-7566

Foundation Roundtable
c/o Santa Barbara Foundation
15 East Carrillo Street
Santa Barbara, CA 93101

Grantmakers of Oregon and Southwest Washington
621 SW Morrison, Suite 725
Portland, OR 97205
Ph: (503) 241-4947
Fax: (503) 248-1126

Greenville Area Donors Forum (SC)
P.O. Box 6906
Greenville, SC 29606
Ph: (864) 233-5925
Fax: (864) 242-9292

The Hui of Grantmakers
c/o Hawaii Community Foundation
900 Fort Street, Suite 1300
Honolulu, HI 96813
Ph: (808) 537-6333
Fax: (808) 521-6286

Iowa Council of Foundations
c/o R. J. McElroy Trust
500 East 4th Street, Suite 318
Waterloo, IA 50703
Ph: (319) 291-1299

Jacksonville Donors Forum
112 W. Adams, Suite 114
Jacksonville, FL 32202
Ph: (904) 356-4483
Fax: (904) 356-7910

Maine Grantmakers Association
210 Main Street
Ellsworth, ME 04605
Ph: (207) 667-9735
Fax: (207) 667-9738

Memphis Grantmakers Forum
6077 Primacy Parkway, Suite 230
Memphis, TN 38119
Ph: (901) 761-9180
Fax: (901) 761-0237

Mobile Private Foundation Forum
PO Box 990
Mobile, AL 36601-0990
Ph: (334) 438-5591
Fax: (334) 438-5592

New Hampshire Charitable Foundation
37 Pleasant Street
Concord, NH 03301-4005
Ph: (603) 225-6641
Fax: (603) 225-1700

New Orleans Area Grantmakers
c/o The Greater New Orleans Foundation
2515 Canal Street, Suite 401
New Orleans, LA 70119
Ph: (504) 822-4906
Fax: (504) 821-8326

Southern Regional Council
133 Carnegie Way, Suite 900
Atlanta, GA 30303-1024
Ph: (404) 522-8764
Fax: (404) 522-8791

Triangle Donors Forum (NC)
P.O. Box 12834
Research Triangle, NC 27709
Ph: (919) 549-9840
Fax: (919) 990-9066

West Virginia Grantmakers, Inc.
P.O. Box 3041
Charleston, WV 25331
Ph: (304) 246-3620
Fax: (304) 346-3640

Western New York Grantmakers Association
712 Main Street
Buffalo, NY 14202-1720
Ph: (716) 845-0734
Fax: (716) 852-2861

Special Interest Grantmaking Associations (U.S.)

Asian Americans/Pacific Islanders in Philanthropy

To inform the philanthropic community about critical and emerging issues in the Asian Pacific Islander community, to increase Asian Pacific Islander representation on boards of trustees and staff of philanthropic organizations, and to increase the ability of Asian Pacific Islander nonprofits to access philanthropic funds.
116 East 16th Street, 7th floor
New York, NY 10003
Ph: (212) 260-3999
Fax: (212) 260-4546
E-mail: AAPIP@aol.com

Association of Black Foundation Executives

To encourage increased grantmaking that addresses issues and problems facing African Americans, and to promote the status and number of African Americans in philanthropy.
550 West North Street, Suite 301
Indianapolis, IN 46202
Ph: (317) 684-8905
Fax: (317) 684-2128

Association of Small Foundations

To provide an opportunity for small foundations to discuss concerns related to quality foundation operations with just a director or small staff.

733 15th Street NW, Suite 700
Washington, DC 20005
Ph: (202) 393-4433
Fax: (202) 393-4474
E-mail: asf@erols.com

Communications Network in Philanthropy

To enhance the professional skills and effectiveness of members and to raise awareness of communications benefits within the philanthropic community.
c/o Benton Foundation
1634 Eye Street NW
Washington, DC 20006
Ph: (202) 638-5770
Fax: (202) 638-5771

Disability Funders Network

To share information on grantmaking opportunities and current developments related to people with disabilities, and to promote the inclusion of people with disabilities in the field of philanthropy.
c/o The Dole Foundation for Employment of People with Disabilities
1819 H Street NW, Suite 340
Washington, DC 20006
Ph: (202) 457-0318
Fax: (202) 457-0473

Environmental Grantmakers Association

To promote recognition that the environment and its inhabitants are endangered by unsustainable human activities, to facilitate communication and cooperation among our members and potential members, and to increase the resources available to address environmental concerns.
c/o The Rockefeller Family Fund
1290 Avenue of the Americas, Room 3450
New York, NY 10104
Ph: (212) 373-4260
Fax: (212) 315-0996

Forum on Religion, Philanthropy and Public Life
To understand relationships and increase alliances among foundations and organized philanthropy.
c/o Maurice Falk Medical Fund
3315 Grant Building
Pittsburgh, PA 15219-2395
Ph: (412) 261-2485
Fax: (412) 471-7739

Funders' Committee for Citizen Participation
To encourage more attention and support of the broad issues of citizen engagement, both electorally and in society.
c/o The Rockefeller Family Fund
1290 Avenue of the Americas
New York, NY 10104
Ph: (212) 373-4252
Fax: (212) 315-0996

Funders Concerned About AIDS
To mobilize philanthropic resources and leadership domestically and internationally to eradicate AIDS and address the social and economic consequences.
50 East 42nd Street, 19th Floor
New York, NY 10017
Ph: (212) 573-5533
Fax: (212) 949-1672

Grantmakers in Aging
To stimulate interest among foundations and corporations in the current issues, programs, and policies that affect older people; to provide information about the grant-making opportunities in the field of aging; to facilitate collaborative grantmaking among member organizations and when appropriate government agencies.
c/o The Philanthropic Group
630 Fifth Avenue, 20th Floor
New York, NY 10111-0254
Ph: (212) 877-2050
Fax: (212) 501-7788

Grantmakers in the Arts

To strengthen arts philanthropy and its role in contributing to a supportive environment for the arts nationwide.
c/o Humboldt Area Foundation
P.O. Box 99
Bayside, CA 95524
Ph: (707) 442-2993
Fax: (707) 442-3811

Grantmakers for Children, Youth and Families

To increase the effectiveness and capacity of grantmakers to improve the well-being of and opportunities for children, youth and families.
815 15th Street, NW, Suite 801
Washington, DC 20005
Ph: (202) 393-6714
Fax: (202) 393-4148

Grantmakers Concerned with Care at the End of Life

c/o Open Society Institute
888 Seventh Avenue, 31st Floor
New York, NY 10106
Ph: (212) 548-0600
Fax: (212) 887-3890

Grantmakers Concerned with Immigrants and Refugees

To promote awareness and understanding among funders about issues concerning newcomers, immigration, refugee trends, and public policy; to facilitate the sharing of information on these issues among grantmakers; and to increase financial support for projects and activities concerned with immigrants and refugees.
c/o Open Society Institute
888 Seventh Avenue
New York, NY 10106
Ph: (212) 887-0167
Fax: (212) 245-3429

Grantmakers for Education

To improve educational outcomes for students by strengthening philanthropy's capacity and effectiveness.

c/o Rockefeller Foundation
420 Fifth Avenue
New York, NY 10018
Ph: (212) 969-8500
Fax: (212) 852-8203

Grantmaking for Effective Organizations
c/o David and Lucile Packard Foundation
300 Second Street, Suite 200
Los Altos, CA 94022
Ph: (415) 948-7658
Fax: (415) 948-5793

Grantmakers Evaluation Network
To provide a forum and network for philanthropists interested in evaluation.
c/o David and Lucile Packard Foundation
300 Second Street, Suite 200
Los Altos, CA 94022
Ph: (415) 948-7658
Fax: (415) 948-5793

Grantmakers in Film, Television and Video
To promote awareness and understanding of the ways "motion media" (film, television, video, and the newer digital technologies such as CD-ROM and the Web) can enhance effective grantmaking.
c/o National Video Resources
73 Spring Street, #606
New York, NY 10012
Ph: (212) 274-8080
Fax: (212) 274-8081

Grantmakers Forum on Community and National Service
Haley Mortimor, Project Manager
444 DeHaro Street, Suite 202
San Francisco, CA 94107
Ph: (415) 522-5400
Fax: (415) 522-5445

Grantmakers in Health

To enhance the health and well-being of all people. In pursuing its mission, GIH works to: educate and inform the private sector grantmaking community about the content and implications of current and emerging health and human services issues; and to foster communication, interaction, and information exchange among grantmakers.
c/o Jewish Healthcare Foundation
Centre City Tower
650 Smithfield Street, Suite 2330
Pittsburgh, PA 15222
Ph: (412) 261-1400

Grantmakers Income Security Task Force

To promote understanding of income security issues among funders and to advance collaborative strategies in this area.
c/o The Ford Foundation
320 East 43rd Street
New York, NY 10017
Ph: (212) 573-5000
Fax: (212) 599-4584

Grants Managers Network

To provide a forum to exchange information about grants management and its relevance to efficient and effective grantmaking.
c/o Carnegie Corporation of New York
437 Madison Ave
New York, NY 10022
Ph: (212) 207-6225
Fax: (212) 754-4073

Grantmakers in Support of Reproductive Rights

c/o Robert Sterling Clark Foundation
112 East 64th Street
New York, NY 10021
Ph: (212) 288-8900
Fax: (212) 288-1033

Hispanics in Philanthropy

To advocate for increased philanthropic support of Latino communities and greater representation of Latinos on the board and staff of foundations.

Diana Campoamor, President
2606 Dwight Way
Berkeley, CA 94704
Ph: (510) 649-1690
Fax: (510) 649-1692

National Network of Grantmakers
To maintain a network of grantmakers who support social change issues and to advocate for change inside and outside the philanthropic community.
1717 Kettner Boulevard, Suite 110
San Diego, CA 92101
Ph: (619) 231-1348
Fax: (619) 231-1349
E-mail: nng@nng.org

Native Americans in Philanthropy
To increase the understanding and presence of organized philanthropy in native communities and to serve as a bridge between native people and organized philanthropy.
P.O. Drawer 1429
1102 1/2 East Second Street
Lumberton, NC 28359
Ph: (910) 618-9749
Fax: (910) 618-9839
E-mail: nap@vacationtime.net

National Office on Philanthropy and the Black Church
Audrey Daniel, Director
1090 Vermont Avenue NW, Suite 1100
Washington, DC 20005-4961
Ph: (202) 789-3530
Fax: (202) 789-3517

Neighborhood Funders Group
The Neighborhood Funders Group is a membership association of grantmaking institutions. Our mission is to strengthen the capacity of organized philanthropy to understand and support community-based efforts to organize and improve the economic and social fabric of low-income urban neighborhoods and rural communities. We provide information, learning opportunities, and other professional development activities to our national membership, and

encourage the support of policies and practices that advance economic and social justice.
6862 Elm Street, Suite 320
McLean, VA 22101
Ph: (703) 448-1777
Fax: (703) 448-1780
E-mail: nfgoffice@aol.com

Project on Death in America
c/o Open Society Institute
888 Seventh Avenue, 31st Floor
New York, NY 10106
Ph: (212) 757-2323
Fax: (212) 974-0367

Southern Africa Grantmakers
To facilitate communication and collaboration among grantmakers with interest in southern Africa, and to increase private grantmaking in the region.
c/o The Henry J. Kaiser Family Foundation
1450 G Street NW, Suite 250
Washington, DC 20005
Ph: (202) 347-5270
Fax: (202) 347-5274

Working Group on Funding Lesbian and Gay Issues
To increase the philanthropic community's knowledge, understanding, and awareness of critical funding needs on the gay, lesbian, and bisexual communities; to encourage increased representation within the foundations at the staff and trustee level of people with diverse sexual identities; and to educate communities and organizations serving these populations about philanthropy and how to access philanthropic resources.
116 East 16th Street, 7th Floor
New York, NY 10003
Ph: (212) 475-2930
Fax: (212) 982-3321

Foreign and International Associations of Grantmakers

Europe

Association of Charitable Foundations
4 Bloomsbury Square
London WC1A 2RL
England
Ph: 44-171-404-1338
Fax: 44-171-831-3881
E-mail: nsiederer@acf.org.uk

Association of Community Trusts and Foundations
4 Bloomsbury Square
London WC1A 2RL
England
Ph: 44-171-831-0033
Fax: 44-171-831-3881

Bundesverband Deutscher Stiftungen E.V.
(Association of German Foundations)
Adenauerallee 15
Bonn 1
Germany
Ph: 49-228-21-8031
Fax: 49-228-21-4526

Centro Español de Fundaciones
Valle Don Ramón de la Cruz 36, 2A
28015 Madrid
Spain
Ph: 34-91-576-1687, 577-6144
Fax: 34-91-576-1601

Confederacion Española de Fundaciones
Ortega y Gasset, N. 20,
3a Planta 28006
Madrid Spain
Ph: 34-1-578-2585
Fax: 34-1-578-3623

Coordinadora Catalana De Fundaciones
Passeig de Gracia 69,
5 planta, Despatx 23
08008 Barcelona Spain
Ph: 34-3487-0130 ext. 23
Fax: 34-3215-1766

Czech Donors' Forum
Karoliny Svetle 4
110 00 Prague 1
Czech Republic
Ph: (420) 226-7230
Fax: (420) 224-228-121

Donors Forum of Russia
c/o Mott Foundation
Zitna 6/8
Prague 2–12000,
Czech Republic
Ph: 2499-3181
Fax: 2499-3183

European Foundation Centre
51 rue de la Concorde
Brussels B-1050
Belgium
Ph: 32-2-512-8938
Fax: 32-2-512-3265
http://www.efc.be

Finnish Council Of Foundations
Bulevardi 5A PL 203
Helsinki 00121
Finland
Ph: 358-0-602-144
Fax: 358-0-640-474

Fondation de France
40 Avenue Hoche 75008
Paris,
France
Ph: 33-144-21-3100/3174
Fax: 33-144-21-3101

170

Portuguese Foundation Centre
c/o FUNDAÇAO ORIENTE
Rua do Salitre, 62
1250 Lisbon
Portugal
Ph: 351-1-353-8280
Fax: 351-1-353-8285

Schweizerische Arbeitsgemeinschaft Kultereller Stiftungen
c/o Jubilaeums Stiftung
Bahnhofstrasse 4
8021 Zurich
Switzerland

Netherlands Association of Foundations
Jan Van Nassaustraat 102
2596 BW The Hague
The Netherlands
Ph: 31-70-326-2753
Fax: 31-70-326-2229

Slovak Donors Forum
c/o Nadacia pre deti a mladez
Hviezdoslavovo nam.17
8111 02 Bratislava,
Slovakia

Stifterverband für die Deutsche Wissenschaft
Barkhovenallee 1/POB 164460
45239/4522 Essen,
Germany
Ph: 49-201-840-10
Fax: 49-201-840-1301

Third Sector Foundation of Turkey
Cemil Topuzlu Caddesi
Karaoman Apt. 68/3
81080 Istanbul
Turkey
Ph: 90-216-302-4535

Asia

Center for Philanthropy and Civil Society
118 Klong-Chan
Bankapi
Bangkok 10240
Thailand
Ph: 66-2-3777206
Fax: 66-2-3747399

The Federation of Korean Industries
28-1 Youido-dong,
Yeongdungopo-ku
Seoul,
Korea
Ph: 82-2-3771-0114
Fax: 82-2-3771-0138/0110

Indian Center for Philanthropy
10 Amaltas Marg
DLF Qutab Enclave
Phase 1 Gurgaon, Haryana
India
Ph: (91) 124-351862
Fax: (91) 113-716656
http://www.icpindia.org/

Japan Foundation Center
YKB Shinjuku-gyoen Building
1-3-8 Shinjuku, Shinjuku-ku
Tokyo 160
Japan
Ph: (81) 3-3350-1857
Fax: (81) 3-3350-1858

League of Corporate Foundations (Lcf)
3/F, Metro South Coop Bank Building
Manila
Philippines
Ph: 632-897-9043 (44)
Fax: 632-897-9054

172

Philippine Business for Social Progress
3F Philippine Social
Development Centre Building
Magallanes Cor. Real Streets,
Intramuros
Manila
Philippines
Ph: 632-527-7741 to 50
Fax: 632-527-3743, 527-3851

Prip Trust
House # 59A
Satmasjid Road, Dhanmondi R/A
Dhaka Bangladesh

Australia/New Zealand

Philanthropy New Zealand
P.O. Box 1521
296 Lambton Quay
Wellington
New Zealand
Ph: 64-4-499-4090
Fax: 64-4-472-5367

Philanthropy Australia, Inc.
Level 3, 111 Collins Street
Melbourne, Victoria 3000
Australia
Ph: 61-3-9650-9255
Fax: 61-3-9654-8298
http://www.philanthropy.org.au

Africa

Southern Africa Grantmakers Association (SAGA)
P.O. Box 31667
Braamfontein 2017
South Africa
Ph: 27-11-403-1610
Fax: 27-11-403-1689

Caribbean

Jamaican Foundations and Corporate Donors (JFCD)
c/o ICWI Group Foundation
2 St. Lucia Avenue,
Kingston 5
Jamaica, WI
Ph: 809-929-1725/876-926-9040, ext. 2407
Fax: 876-968-8056

North America

The Conference Board of Canada
The Canadian Centre for Business in the Community
255 Smyth Road
Ottawa, Ontario
Canada KIH 8M7
Ph: (613) 526-3280
Fax: (613) 526-1747

Canadian Centre for Philanthropy
425 University Avenue, Suite #700
Toronto, Ontario,
Canada M5G 1T6
Ph: (416) 597-2293 ext. 222
Fax: (416) 597-2294
http://www.ccp.ca

Centro Mexicano para la Filantropía
Mazatlán No. 96
Col. Condesa
México, D.F. 06140
Ph: 525-256-3739, 235-3762
Fax: 525-256-3190
http://www.cemefi.org

Community Foundations of Canada
75 Albert Street Suite 301
Ottawa, Ontario
Canada KIP 5E7
Ph: (613) 236-2664
Fax: (613) 236-1621

Council on Foundations
1828 L St., Suite 300
Washington, DC 20036
USA
Ph: (202) 467-0380
Fax: (202) 466-5722

Independent Sector
1828 L Street, N.W.
Washington, DC 20036
Ph: (202) 223-8100
Fax: (202) 416-0580
http://www.indepsec.org

South America

Group Of Institutes, Foundations and Enterprises (GIFE)
Alameda Ribeirão Preto,
130 – j. 12
01331–000
São Paulo – SP
Brazil
Ph: 55-11-287-2349
Fax: 55-11-287-2349

Grupo de Fundaciones
25 de Mayo 501
(1002) Buenos Aires
Argentina
Ph: (541) 318-6610
Fax: (541) 318-6611

Appendix E

Community Foundations

Alaska
Alaska Conservation Foundation

Arkansas
Foundation for the Mid South

California
California Community Foundation
Community Foundation of Riverside County
Community Foundation of Santa Cruz County
Community Foundation of Silicon Valley
Glendale Community Foundation
Humboldt Area Foundation
Marin Community Foundation
North Valley Community Foundation
Peninsula Community Foundation
San Diego Community Foundation
The San Francisco Foundation
Sonoma Community Foundation
Sonora Area Foundation

Connecticut
Hartford Foundation for Public Giving

Community Foundations

Florida
The Community Foundation for Palm Beach And Martin Counties
The Community Foundation of Sarasota County

Indiana
Central Indiana Community Foundation

Illinois
The Aurora Foundation

Kansas
Greater Kansas City Community Foundation

Louisiana
Foundation for the Mid South

Maine
Maine Community Foundation

Maryland
Community Foundation of the Eastern Shore

Michigan
Community Foundation of Greater Flint
Greater Rochester Area Community Foundation
The Community Foundation for Muskegon County
Saginaw Community Foundation

Minnesota
The Minneapolis Foundation

Mississippi
Foundation for the Mid South

Missouri
Greater Kansas City Community Foundation

Nebraska
Grand Island Community Foundation
Lincoln Community Foundation

New Jersey
Princeton Area Community Foundation

New Mexico
Albuquerque Community Foundation

New York
Northern Chautauqua Community Foundation
Rochester Area Community Foundation

North Carolina
Community Foundation of Greater Greensboro
Foundation for the Carolinas
Triangle Community Foundation

Ohio
The Columbus Foundation
The Community Foundation of Greater Lorain County
Parkersburg Area Community Foundation

Pennsylvania
The Philadelphia Foundation

Puerto Rico
Puerto Rico Community Foundation

South Carolina
The Community Foundation Serving Coastal South Carolina
Foundation tor the Carolinas

Texas
Kerrville Area Community Trust
Lubbock Area Foundation, Inc.
San Antonio Area Foundation

West Virginia
Parkersburg Area Community Foundation

Wisconsin
The Milwaukee Foundation

Wyoming
Community Foundation of Jackson Hole

Sample Funding Guidelines Information Sheet

The Phil N. Thropist Foundation
P.O. Box CC
Charityville, CA 91234
(123) 555-0767

1999 Funding Guidelines

1999 Funding Priorities

For the 1999 fiscal year, The Phil N. Thropist Foundation will focus its funding in the following three areas as they relate to the youth of the Somewhere Valley community:

- Leadership building
- Mentoring
- Educational/vocational motivation

Requests to fund programs benefiting youth of Polish-American heritage are especially encouraged.

Funding Eligibility

The Thropist Foundation will consider applications submitted by individuals, nonprofit organizations, and public agencies. Funds may be requested for the following purposes:

- Acquisition of equipment necessary to the implementation of an eligible program or service
- Development or implementation of a new program or service addressing one of the three focus areas
- Maintenance of an ongoing program or service in one of the three focus areas

Scholarships

In addition, the Thropist Foundation will continue to provide scholarship aid to students from throughout the Somewhere Valley wishing to continue or further their education at an academic or vocational institution. Students of Polish-American heritage are particularly encouraged to apply.

Limitations

The Foundation will not consider granting funds in 1999 for:

- Endowment purposes
- General operating expenses
- Underwriting of fundraising events

Although scholarship funds will be available for students from throughout the Somewhere Valley, the Thropist Foundation has elected to provide grant funding only for programs and services benefiting Somewhere Valley populations residing east of Washington Street.

Funding requests must fall within the range of $250 to $5,000, with the largest grants reserved for programs of extraordinary impact on the target community.

The Thropist Foundation will look most favorably upon funding requests for matching and challenge grants.

Application Procedures

1. Complete and return the Application for Funding (please follow instructions carefully)
2. For requests of $1,000 or more, also provide:
   - Program budget, including projected sources of funding
   - List of Board of Directors and their affiliations
   - Financial statement for the most recently completed fiscal year (if unavailable, please provide the most recently submitted Form 990)

Please do not submit any additional materials unless specifically requested to do so by the Thropist Foundation.

Review Process

The grant review process may take up to four months from the time your proposal is received. Therefore, proposals should be submitted at least four months prior to the start of the proposed grant period.

Applicants are encouraged to communicate with the Thropist Foundation prior to submitting a proposal to ensure that the proposed project meets the interests and guidelines of the Foundation.

Appendix G

Sample Funding Application

The Phil N. Thropist Foundation
Application for Funding

(Please type or print)

1. Organization Submitting Proposal

   Name: _____

   Street Address: _____

   City/State/ZIP: _____

   Telephone: _____

   Fax: _____

2. Organization Head

   Name: _____ Title: _____

3. Contact (if other than above)

   Name: _____ Title: _____

Sample Funding Application

4. Program or Project Name: _____

5. Total Program Budget: _____

6. Amount of Funding Request: _____

7. Period for Which Funding is Sought: _____

8. Under which of the 1998 Thropist Foundation funding priorities does this project fall?

  _____ Leadership building

  _____ Mentoring

  _____ Educational/vocational motivation

9. Under which of the funding eligibility guidelines does it fall?

  _____ Acquisition of equipment necessary to the implementation of an eligible program or service

  _____ Development or implementation of a new program or service addressing one of the three focus areas

  _____ Maintenance of an ongoing program or service in one of the three focus areas

Please answer all questions within the space provided. Do not attach additional pages.

10. Briefly outline the basic structure of your proposed program:

11. What specific problem or issue does this program seek to address?

Name of Applicant Organization: _____

12. What are the specific goals of the program, and how will you determine whether those goals have been met? For an existing program or service, how has success in meeting goals been measured in the past?

13. How will the applicant organization maintain funding for this program or service once the Thropist Foundation has completed its support?

14. Briefly and candidly, describe the quality and commitment of the applicant organization's Board of Directors

15. What percentage of the Board made a financial contribution to the organization in the last fiscal year?

16. Briefly and candidly, describe the overall fiscal health of the applicant organization.

Name of Applicant Organization: _____

17. What other funders (e.g., individuals, corporations, business-es, foundations) have supported this organization over the last twelve months with either financial or in-kind contributions?

    Name: Amount:

18. How will a grant from the Thropist Foundation be used to attract additional funding for this program or service?

19. Who from outside the organization can be contacted as a reference for this program?

    Name: Title:

    Organization:

    Telephone:

20. Please highlight any unique or innovative aspects of your proposed program or project:

    a.

    b.

    c.

    d.

    e.

Name of Applicant Organization: _____

Ten Key Questions Every Board Member Should Be Able to Answer

Developed by Rafferty Consulting Group, © 1993

1. How long is the organization's mission statement and what does it say?

2. What are the organization's three main goals for the next two years?

3. How do your organization's programs and services compare with those of other organizations similar in mission, size, and budget? How do they differ?

4. What is your organization's fundraising goal for this year? What portion of that goal do you feel personally responsible for?

5. In your last fiscal year, did donated funds increase or decrease compared with the year before? In your current fiscal year, are donated funds increasing or decreasing compared with last year?

6. Approximately how many volunteers regularly work on behalf of the organization? How are they recognized or rewarded?

7. When was the last time your organization had a significant mention in the local or general media? When was the last time your organization had a significant mention in a professional or trade publication?

8. What elements comprise your staff's salary and benefits package? Approximately what is the salary of each of your organization's key administrators?

9. Last fiscal year, did your organization end in the red or in the black? By how much? This fiscal year, are you currently heading to end in the red or in the black? By how much?

10. Specifically, why were you asked to serve on this board?

Donor Bill of Rights

The following Donor Bill of Rights was developed by the major professional associations representing fund development experts and practitioners serving all fields of the charitable sector: The American Association of Fund-Raising Counsel (AAFRC), The Association for Healthcare Philanthropy (AHP), The Council for Advancement and Support of Education (CASE), and The National Society of Fund Raising Executives (NSFRE).

Philanthropy is based on voluntary action for the common good. It is a tradition of giving and sharing that is primary to the quality of life. To assure that philanthropy merits the respect and trust of the general public, and that donors and prospective donors can have full confidence in the not-for-profit organizations and causes they are asked to support, we declare that all donors have these rights:

1. To be informed of the organization's mission, of the way the organization intends to use donated resources, and of its capacity to use donations effectively for their intended purposes.

2. To be informed of the identity of those serving on the organization's governing board, and to expect the board to exercise prudent judgment in its stewardship responsibilities.

3. To have access to the organization's most recent financial statements.

4. To be assured their gifts will be used for the purposes for which they were given.

5. To receive appropriate acknowledgment and recognition.

6. To be assured that information about their donations is handled with respect and with confidentiality to the extent provided by law.

7. To expect that all relationships with individuals representing organizations of interest to the donor will be professional in nature.

8. To be informed whether those seeking donations are volunteers, employees of the organization or hired solicitors.

9. To have the opportunity for their names to be deleted from mailing lists that an organization may intend to share.

10. To feel free to ask questions when making a donation and to receive prompt, truthful and forthright answers.

Model Standards for the Charitable Gift Planner

These standards were adopted and subscribed to by the National Committee on Planned Giving and the American Council on Gift Annuities, May 7, 1991.

Preamble

The purpose of this statement is to encourage responsible charitable gift planning by urging the adoption of the following Standards of Practice by all who work in the charitable gift planning process, including charitable institutions and their gift planning officers, independent fundraising consultants, attorneys, accountants, financial planners and life insurance agents, collectively referred to hereafter as "Gift Planners."

This statement recognizes that the solicitation, planning and administration of a charitable gift is a complex process involving philanthropic, personal, financial, and tax considerations, and often involves professionals from various disciplines whose goals should include working together to structure a gift that achieves a fair and proper balance between the interests of the donor and the purposes of the charitable institution.

I. Primacy of Philanthropic Motivation
The principal basis for making a charitable gift should be a desire on the part of the donor to support the work of charitable institutions.

II. Explanation of Tax Implications
Congress has provided tax incentives for charitable giving, and the emphasis in this statement on philanthropic motivation in no way minimizes the necessity and appropriateness of a full and accurate explanation by the Gift Planner of those incentives and their implications.

III. Full Disclosure
It is essential to the gift planning process that the role and relationships of all parties involved, including how and by whom each is compensated, be fully disclosed to the donor. A Gift Planner shall not act or purport to act as a representative of any charity without the express knowledge and approval of the charity, and shall not, while employed by the charity, act or purport to act as a representative of the donor, without the express consent of both the charity and the donor.

IV. Compensation
Compensation paid to Gift Planners shall be reasonable and proportionate to the services provided. Payment of finders fees, commissions or other fees by a donee organization to an independent Gift Planner as a condition for the delivery of a gift are never appropriate. Such payments lead to abusive practices and may violate certain state and federal regulations. Likewise, commission-based compensation for Gift Planners who are employed by a charitable institution is never appropriate.

V. Competence and Professionalism
The Gift Planner should strive to achieve and maintain a high degree of competence in his or her chosen area, and shall advise

donors only in areas in which he or she is professionally qualified. It is a hallmark of professionalism for Gift Planners that they realize when they have reached the limits of their knowledge and expertise, and as a result, should include other professionals in the process. Such relationships should be characterized by courtesy, tact and mutual respect.

VI. Consultation with Independent Advisers

A Gift Planner acting on behalf of a charity shall in all cases strongly encourage the donor to discuss the proposed gift with competent independent legal and tax advisers of the donor's choice.

VII. Consultation with Charities

Although Gift Planners frequently and properly counsel donors concerning specific charitable gifts without the prior knowledge or approval of the donee organization, the Gift Planners, in order to insure that the gift will accomplish the donor's objectives, should encourage the donor, early in the gift planning process, to discuss the proposed gift with the charity to whom the gift is to be made. In cases where the donor desires anonymity, the Gift Planners shall endeavor, on behalf of the undisclosed donor, to obtain the charity's input in the gift planning process.

VIII. Explanation of the Gift

The Gift Planner shall make every effort, insofar as possible, to insure that the donor receives a full and accurate explanation of all aspects of the proposed charitable gift.

X. Full Compliance

A Gift Planner shall fully comply with and shall encourage other parties in the gift planning process to fully comply with both the letter and spirit of all applicable federal and state laws and regulations.

X. Public Trust

Gift Planners shall, in all dealings with donors, institutions and other professionals, act with fairness, honesty, integrity and openness. Except for compensation received for services, the terms of which have been disclosed to the donor, they shall have no vested interest that could result in personal gain.

Index

About the Author

Renata J. Rafferty is the Founder and Principal of Rafferty Consulting Group. For over two decades, she has assisted individuals, families, and foundations in defining and maintaining a clear focus in their philanthropic activities. Her firm also provides comprehensive consulting, training, and facilitation services for nonprofit and public agencies operating in areas including education, the arts, health, and community and social services.

In her consulting practice, she has assisted clients as diverse as The National Ballet of Canada, The Community Foundation of Riverside County, the Chicago Academy of Science, The Jewish Federation Council of Los Angeles, Pepperdine University, and the National Association for Hispanic Elderly.

Ms. Rafferty has also advised numerous government agencies such as the U.S. Department of Labor, the California State Library system, the Riverside County Office on Aging (Ca), and individual cities and municipalities. Further, she served as special counsel to both the Foreign Investment Agency and the Ministry of Foreign Economic Affairs for the Republic of Poland.

As a nationally recognized presenter, Ms. Rafferty has taught or lectured on philanthropy and charitable sector issues at the Massachusetts Institute of Technology, Georgetown University, Loyola University of Chicago, Webber-Douglas Academy (London), and the University of Southern California Graduate School of Business. She has appeared as a speaker before members of the World Affairs Council in Los Angeles, as well as addressing other national and international associations, conferences, and symposia. In her work overseas, Ms. Rafferty has advised foundations and charities in Eastern Europe and has served on the staff of the Vatican.

She has been profiled in *Inc.* magazine, and writes a weekly column on nonprofit and philanthropic issues for a major Gannett newspaper. Ms. Rafferty is also a lead instructor with the Southern California Center for Nonprofit Management in Los Angeles and co-founded The Nonprofit Leadership Consortium and The Executive Directors' Roundtable, both in Riverside County, California.

Ms. Rafferty holds a Bachelor of Arts degree from Loyola University of Chicago, a Master of Arts degree from Tufts University in Boston, and is a former Fulbright Scholar with the Jagiellonian University in Krakow, Poland.

Rafferty Consulting Group
45-775 Indian Wells Lane
Indian Wells, CA 92210 USA
Ph: (760) 776-9606
Fax: (760) 776-9608
E-mail: raffcons@ix.netcom.com
Web site: http://www.raffertyconsulting.com